Norman T. Carrington MA

Brodie's Notes on William Shakespeare's

Much Ado about Nothing

Pan Books London and Sydney

First published by James Brodie Ltd
This edition published 1976 by Pan Books Ltd
Cavaye Place, London SW10 9PG
6 7 8 9

ISBN 0 330 50036 8
Filmset in Great Britain by
Northumberland Press Ltd, Gateshead, Tyne and Wear
Printed and bound by
Richard Clay (The Chaucer Press) Ltd, Bungay, Suffolk

Contents

The author and his work 5

The Elizabethan theatre 8

The text of Shakespeare's plays 12

Plot, source and treatment 13

Theme, atmosphere and setting 18

Structure and style 23

Characters 29

Scene summaries, textual notes and revision questions 47

General questions 78

Line references in these Notes are to the Oxford University Press edition of *Shakespeare: Complete Works*, but as references are also given to particular Acts and Scenes, the Notes may be used with any edition of the play

To the student

A close reading of the play is the student's primary task, but it is well worth seeing a performance if possible. These Notes will help to increase your understanding and appreciation of the play, and to stimulate *your own* thinking about it: *they are in no way intended as a substitute* for a thorough knowledge of the play.

The author and his work

Surprisingly little is known of the life of our greatest dramatist, and the little we can be sure about comes mainly from brief references to him in legal or other formal documents. Though there is no record of Shakespeare's actual birth date, we do know that he was christened William at the market town of Stratford-on-Avon on 26 April 1564. He was the third child of John Shakespeare – variously described as glover, wool dealer, farmer and butcher – and Mary Arden, whose family were prosperous local landowners. However, until the year 1578, when his business began to decline, John Shakespeare was a notable figure in Stratford, and William was probably educated at the local grammar school – where he would have learned the 'small Latin and less Greek' of which the playwright Ben Jonson (1572–1637) accused him. But John Aubrey (1626–97) in his *Brief Lives* (written in the seventeenth century but not published until 1813) says that Shakespeare had 'enough education to become a schoolmaster' – and stated categorically that his father was *not* a butcher.

In 1582, at the age of eighteen, Shakespeare married Anne Hathaway, a woman eight years his senior, who bore him two girls and a boy: Susanna in 1583 and the twins Hamnet and Judith in 1585. He is thought to have left Stratford for London in 1585: there is a tradition (which Aubrey does not deny) that Shakespeare had to flee his native town to avoid prosecution for stealing deer in Sir Thomas Lucy's grounds. But, more to the point, it seems that he left with a band of strolling players, the Queen's Players, who visited Stratford in 1585.

Whether he took his wife and children with him to London is not known, but a pamphlet published in 1592 by a lesser playwright Robert Greene mentions Shakespeare as an actor and playwright. Plague caused the theatres to close in 1593; on their reopening in the following year we know that Shakespeare was by then a member of The Lord Chamberlain's Company (known after the accession of James I as The King's Men). It is probable that he stayed with this company throughout the remainder of his career, writing plays and acting in them in various theatres. His connection with the company must have brought him considerable financial reward, and

Shakespeare seems to have been a good businessman as well, for when he retired to Stratford in 1611, aged forty-seven, he was already a fairly wealthy man and a shareholder in two theatres, the Globe and the Blackfriars. He purchased New Place, one of the largest houses in Stratford – where he entertained Ben Jonson and the poet Michael Drayton (1563–1631), and – by the astute purchase of tithes and arable land – he became, in the tradition of his maternal forefathers, a prosperous landowner. He died in Stratford-on-Avon on 23 April 1616, survived by his wife and two daughters.

As an actor Shakespeare does not seem to have been particularly successful; but even in his own day his fame as a dramatist and his personal popularity were great. In 1598 Francis Meres (1567–1647), the writer of critical assessments of playwrights, described Shakespeare as 'the most excellent in both kinds' [i.e. in comedy and in tragedy], and even Ben Jonson, whose dramatic work was in a very different vein, remarks of Shakespeare in *Discoveries* (published posthumously in 1640), 'I lov'd the man and do honour his memory (on this side idolatry) as much as any.' And John Milton (1608–74) wrote in his poem 'l'Allegro' (1632) the often-quoted lines: 'Or sweetest Shakespeare fancy's child/Warble his native woodnotes wild.'

Shakespeare probably began his work as a dramatist by collaborating with others and patching up old plays for his company to revive. His first completely original play is believed to be *Love's Labour's Lost* (?1590), though the date of each play presents a problem: the dates are not given in the First Folio (the first collected edition of his plays, 1623). His first narrative poems, composed during the Plague when the theatres were closed, were *Venus and Adonis* (1593) and *The Rape of Lucrece* (1594). His 154 *Sonnets* were published in 1609 – without Shakespeare's permission, it is said. The first 126 of these intensely personal poems are addressed to a young man, the poet's friend and patron; the remainder to a 'dark lady'. The identity of neither of these two inspirers of the sonnets has been established – nor has it been decided how far the series is autobiographical.

Most of the plays were written for performance in the public playhouses, and were conveniently classified in the First Folio in three groups: comedies, histories and tragedies. But these divisions are too arbitrary – the 'comedies' can contain tragedy, the 'tragedies' moments of mirth, and the 'histories' have aspects of both tragedy and comedy.

When, however, the plays are considered chronologically they fall naturally into four periods. From about **1590–93** Shakespeare was **learning his trade** while patching up existing plays and beginning to write his own: to this period belong *Love's Labour's Lost*, *The Comedy of Errors*, *Two Gentlemen of Verona*, the three *Parts* of *Henry VI*, *Romeo and Juliet* and *Richard III*.

From about **1594–1600** was the period of Shakespeare's **greatest development**, when he wrote such plays as *Titus Andronicus*, *A Midsummer Night's Dream*, *The Merchant of Venice*, *The Taming of the Shrew*, the two *Parts* of *Henry IV*, *The Merry Wives of Windsor*, *As You Like It* and *Twelfth Night*.

Despite what we have said above, the period between **1602–08** can be described as that of **the tragedies**, which include **Hamlet**, *Othello*, *King Lear*, *Macbeth* and *Antony and Cleopatra*.

Shakespeare's **final period (1610–13)** includes three romances: *The Tempest*, *Cymbeline* and *The Winter's Tale*; and one historical play, *Henry VIII*.

As for the original production of these plays, Shakespeare cared little about the dress of his characters – irrespective of place or period, the actors wore the English fashions of his time. And, whatever might be a play's geographical setting, his clowns and lower-class characters were true London cockneys or British country bumpkins – such as would appeal to the gallery in English playhouses.

Since that time, there have been many fashions in 'dressing' the plays: there have been attempts at contemporaneous setting and clothes – in more recent times some of the plays have been produced against stark backgrounds and in modern dress. But today there is a movement towards vaguely 'historical' dress, and (after decades of sonorous, sometimes pompous and often unintelligible speaking of the lines) to a simpler, more naturalistic delivery, such as Shakespeare's original players probably used. But, notwithstanding the many and various innovations over the years, Shakespeare's genius, his lyrical lines and wonderful choice of words, his warmth and his understanding of the human predicament, continue to bring entertainment and enlightenment to people all over the world.

The Elizabethan theatre

At the time of Shakespeare there were probably no more than five public theatres in the land, all in London, and they were built according to the design of contemporary inn-yards, which had been found marvellously convenient places for the presentation of plays.

The theatre was circular or octagonal in shape. The main part of the auditorium was the large round pit, open to the sky, in which the poorer people *stood* (the 'groundlings'). Encircling this, round the walls, were three balconies, covered on top but not in front (like the 'stands' on a football ground), and containing seats. The price of admission to the pit was one Elizabethan penny, while proportionately higher charges were made for the balconies. When it was wet the performance was postponed until the next day.

The stage was large, jutting far into the pit, and was without scenery and any but the most meagre properties. Hence it made no difference that people stood at the side of the stage as well as in front. The scenery was created in the imagination of the audience by the words of the characters in the play: it was made part of the play, so as not to obtrude and destroy the illusion of reality (e.g. III,1,4–11).

The play went straight on without intervals. Lack of intervals and frequent changes of scene were immaterial when the stage was without scenery, consequently a succession of short scenes, as in Act III, is quite common in Elizabethan drama. In a modern play with change of scenery the audience would become impatient at the constant delays. There is good reason to believe that when they were first produced the plays took considerably less time than they do today. The Prologue to *Romeo and Juliet*, for instance, refers to 'the two hours' traffic of our stage'.

In the absence of curtains the end of a scene was frequently marked by rhyming lines, but as there is so little poetry in *Much Ado about Nothing* this is not noticeable. The rhyming couplet at the end of the main part of Act III,1 (105–6) may be to mark the end or possibly to give it the clinching effect of a proverb. The main part of Act IV,1 ends in four lines rhyming alternately (250–3). Remember that Shakespeare did not divide his plays into acts and scenes (see p.12) and that what seems the end of only a part of a scene as printed in our editions may well have appeared the end of a separate episode to him, as here.

Just as the scenery had to be *put into* the play, so had entrances and exits to be arranged as *part of* the play. In a modern play an actor can get into position before the rise of the curtain, but on the open stage it would seem artificial if he walked on and then started his first speech, or finished the scene and then walked off. Such endings as these in the three scenes of the first act clear the stage and at the same time fit in perfectly naturally with the action of the play – 'In practice let us put it presently'; 'Go you with me, and I will use your skill'; '*Don John.* Shall we go prove what's to be done? *Borachio.* We'll wait upon your lordship.' It follows that dead bodies always had to be carried off the stage in the action of the play.

It was not unknown for the stage floor to be equipped with a trap-door for the sudden appearance and disappearance of ghosts and spirits.

At the back of the stage was a recess ('within') and this was curtained and could be shut off when desired. The recess no doubt served for the arbour into which Benedick withdrew in Act II,3, and 'the pleached bower' into which Beatrice stole in Act III,1 (entering the stage from behind). Both came '*forward*' when they were left on their own. There would Borachio and Conrade 'stand close', under the 'pent-house' (III,3), and probably the recess also served for Hero's 'tomb' (V,3).

Above the recess was a balcony, which served for an upper room, castle walls and suchlike scenes. This, too, could be curtained off. No use is made of the balcony in *Much Ado about Nothing*.

People who wanted to be in the public eye were able to hire stools actually on the stage itself. Payment of one shilling extra entitled them to have their pipes lit by a page, thus showing to all and sundry that they were in a position to be attended. Such a privilege would be valued by country gentlemen who wanted it to be known that they had come up to town. It was a source of continual annoyance to playwrights that actors 'gagged' in order to please these aristocratic playgoers.

By law, women were not allowed to act. Consequently women's parts had to be taken by boys with unbroken voices. Considering the limited emotional range of a boy's voice, imagine a boy's rendering of Lady Macbeth or Cleopatra, or even Hero or Beatrice! The ban on actresses accounts for the few women's parts in plays of the period, though some were always introduced for the sake of variety. In *Much Ado about Nothing* there are but four, and this is more than usual in Shakespeare's plays. It also accounts for the large number of plays where a woman disguises herself as a page boy. It made it much easier for the producer; further, the audience was intrigued by a situation in which a character was pretending to be what he really was! In *The Merchant of Venice* every one of the women disguises herself as a man.

Plays were not acted in period costume. Thus all Shakespeare's plays were first acted in 'modern dress'. In considering their suitability for presentation in modern dress today, however, it must not be forgotten that the language of the plays fits in with the Elizabethan costume worn by actors originally. Although there was no scenery, managers spared no expense on the most lavish of costumes.

On days when the theatre was open a flag was flown from the turret, and when the play was about to begin a trumpet was sounded.

The text of Shakespeare's plays

Few readers of Shakespeare realize the difficulties scholars have had to overcome in order to establish accurate texts of the plays. The First Folio (see p.6) contained thirty-six plays. Other large-size collected editions or Folios, were published in the seventeenth century, the Third and Fourth Folios containing seven additional plays, none of which, with the exception of *Pericles*, is now thought to be by Shakespeare. Sixteen of the plays had already been published separately as Quartos (editions half folio size) before 1623, and in the case of some plays, for example, *Hamlet*, more than one Quarto edition exists. Some of these Quartos are almost word for word the same as the texts in the First Folio and were possibly set up from Shakespeare's own manuscript or at least from accurate theatre copies; but others are shortened, inferior versions, possibly 'pirated' editions published by some unauthorized persons who had access to theatre copies or parts of them, or who had taken down the plays in shorthand while they were being performed.

It is thought that the texts of the First Folio were set up from the good Quartos and from good theatre copies. But these texts must all be compared, printers' mistakes and other interference traced, before a reliable text can be arrived at. The first editor to attempt the problem of the text was Nicholas Rowe (1674–1718), who also divided most of the plays into acts and scenes, supplied place-names of the location of each scene, indications of entrances and exits, and lists of dramatis personae, which are absent from many of the texts in the Quarto and Folio editions. The acts only of *Much Ado about Nothing* are indicated in the First Folio. Rowe's scene-divisions are convenient for reference (like the division of the books of the Bible into chapters and verses), but have no important use in Shakespearian study. They were fitted for the stage of Rowe's time, but would have been to no purpose upon Shakespeare's stage with the barest of scenery.

While knowledge of the text is important for examination study, and indeed, intelligent textual study can throw much light on an author, it should never be forgotten that the literary and dramatic aspects of the play are more vital. At the same time, study of the text is the basis of all literary and dramatic study.

Plot, source and treatment

Plot

On his return from the suppression of a rebellion in his principality, Don Pedro stays with Leonato, governor of Messina, bringing with him two of his friends, Claudio and Benedick. Also in their company is Don John, Don Pedro's illegitimate brother, and the leader of the rebellion, with whom, however, he is now reconciled.

Claudio falls in love with Leonato's daughter Hero, and, with their friends' careful contrivance, Hero's cousin Beatrice and Benedick also fall in love, though they are sworn enemies to marriage in general and to one another in particular.

Through the intrigue of Don John, Claudio is led to believe that Hero is false to him, and he repudiates her in public before the altar. But the Watch overhear Don John's aide boasting of his success, and the plot is thus revealed. In the meantime Hero is reported dead through shock. Benedick and Beatrice are drawn closer together by their common support of Hero's reputation. Claudio offers to do penance for his false accusation. The easy 'penance' Leonato imposes is marriage with a niece of his, and, not unnaturally, Claudio agrees to take her. She turns out, however, to be Hero herself, and the play closes with a double wedding, Hero to Claudio, and Beatrice to Benedick. Don John is caught, but is scarcely thought of in the festivities.

Source of plot

Shakespeare 'lifted' the Hero–Claudio story from a translation of the twenty-second 'Novel' of the Italian poet Bandello, introducing Margaret's and Borachio's part's from Spenser's *Faerie Queene* (1590). The Beatrice–Benedick story and the Watch episodes were of Shakespeare's own invention.

Shakespeare was not an original playwright: time and time again he built great works of art out of the well-known stories of his day, which only seem 'Shakespearian' to us because we do not know his minor contemporaries.

Treatment of plot

In essentials Shakespeare's main plot is the same as Bandello's, but there are significant alterations and additions. These illustrate his method. They were obviously deliberate, and were chiefly in the interests of unity of action, or parallelism or contrast. For ease in study they are grouped under separate headings.

Compression of time

Shakespeare compresses the action of twelve months or so in Bandello's novel into a few days, thereby gaining swiftness, power and unity of action.

The action of the play moves according to the following timetable.

First day To and including II,2. Don Pedro and his friends arrive, and a supper in their honour is held the same night. At the masked dance after the supper, Don Pedro conducts Claudio's love affair, Don John purposes to 'cross' it, and Don Pedro to arrange another marriage – between Benedick and Beatrice.

Second day To III,3. The plan to mislead Beatrice is carried out (following the similar deception of Benedick), Don John spreads his lies, and at night the Watch are given their 'charge' and subsequently arrest Borachio and Conrade.

Third day To V,3. The intended wedding-day. Leonato deputes the Watch to examine their prisoner. Claudio rejects Hero in church.

In the afternoon Don Pedro and Claudio come to say goodbye to Leonato. Benedick delivers his challenge. Conrade and Borachio are brought before Leonato and Don John's plot is discovered. Benedick and Beatrice are shown obviously in love. At night Claudio sings his epitaph to Hero's body (she is supposed to have been buried the same day that she died) and agrees to marry her cousin in the morning. This scene ends at dawn.

Fourth day V,4. The play ends with the double wedding.

They are not all necessarily successive days, however. Leonato's original plan was for a week to elapse before the wedding ('Not till

Monday, my dear son, which is hence a just seven-night'). Act II,3 cannot be placed exactly and may have happened on any day in the week before the wedding. On the other hand III,2, where Don John accuses Hero, seems to follow closely on II,2, when he decides to do it. In that case Leonato may have changed his mind about waiting for a week before the wedding, just as Don Pedro changed his mind about staying a month with Leonato.

The student will no doubt be surprised when he sees this time-table set out, for although swift when its time is analysed the play is not so swift in its general impression. The very uncertainty of the particular day on which Benedick was reading in the garden (II,3) has the effect of lengthening the sense of time. In this scene it is said that Beatrice will 'be up twenty times a night', and that Hero is 'sometime afeard she will do a desperate outrage to her-self', as if this has been going on for a considerable time. In III,2, on the day before the wedding, the signs of love in Benedick are implied to be of some days' standing. We hear of 'a fancy that he hath to strange disguises', that 'a' brushes his hat a' mornings' and that his 'jesting spirit' has left him. At the very longest Claudio must have been in love with Hero less than a week, yet Benedick says, 'Now will he lie ten nights awake, carving the fashion of a new doublet'. Thus the impression given is different from what a rigid time analysis would admit if Shakespeare specified the intervals before and after this scene.

In the first scene of the play casual remarks show us that the characters have met before and that some are well acquainted with one another. For instance, we are told that Benedick and Beatrice 'never meet but there's a skirmish of wit between them'. Don Pedro had passed through Messina on his way to the wars and Claudio had seen Hero before. Indeed, we get the impression that Don Pedro was a regular visitor from such a greeting as the following, 'Never came trouble to my house in the likeness of your grace ... but when you depart from me, sorrow abides, and happiness takes his leave'. Only a few hours after Beatrice had first met Don John she says, 'I never can see him but I am heart-burned an hour after'. Thus we are led to believe theirs is a long-standing acquaintance, which makes the events seem more normal and credible, and assists in that 'willing suspension of disbelief' which is necessary to enjoy any fiction.

Similarly, although in actual fact it has been only a few hours since Hero was slandered, Antonio says to Leonato, 'If you go on thus, you will kill yourself'. It is by chance remarks like this that an impression is conveyed of a longer lapse of time than the actual days warrant. In our study of this play the time allowed can be analysed, but Shakespeare's first audiences had no book, and what matters first and foremost in a play is the impression from the stage. Shakespeare constructed his plays without regard for gritty little details, but with much regard for their general pattern.

Unity of place

Shakespeare similarly restricts the scenes of his play as he does the time, again in the interests of unity of effect. Bandello's story goes from Messina to a country house and back again, but Shakespeare confines the action to Messina alone, indeed to the palace and garden of Leonato, the street outside, the church and the gaol.

Additional characters and scenes

When we hear the title *Much Ado about Nothing*, we first think of the Watch, then of Benedick and Beatrice and lastly of Hero and Claudio. The solution to the plot through the intervention of the Watch is entirely Shakespeare's contribution; there was no hint of this in the original, and while Benedick and Beatrice may have been suggested in the first place by two characters in Bandello's 'novel' who are married at the same time as the two main characters, Shakespeare has made them and the parts they play quite different. The 'low comedy' of the Watch and the 'high comedy' of Benedick and Beatrice are introduced for contrast, and for wit and comic relief.

It would be a mistake to think that the borrowing of the outline of the story in any way detracts from Shakespeare's genius. The plot is the least important part of a play. Shakespeare's great artistic power is in characterization, and through it a story which in inferior hands would be crude and improbable becomes real and lifelike. Invention is not the great artistic quality, but insight – the conception the artist has of life as a whole. A story with a 'realistic' plot has no life if the characters are wooden but a crude plot comes to life when living people inhabit it. Artistic creation bears the same relation to plot as architecture to bricks and mortar. Shakespeare was often very careless in his plots; it is in his *use* of the plot that he shows his imagination.

The plot of *Much Ado about Nothing* is no exception. It is very thin at its central point, and the amount learned and acted upon as a result of eavesdropping is incredible. Shakespeare just brushes difficulties aside. For instance, where was Hero when her maid was talking at her window to a man outside between twelve and one o'clock in the morning? 'In the meantime,' says Borachio, nothing doubting of his cleverness, 'I will so fashion the matter that Hero shall be absent.' And it is left at that.

Theme, atmosphere and setting

Theme

The theme of *Much Ado about Nothing* is the power of report, usually false report, 'that only wounds by hearsay' (III,1,23), to alter the course of human life for good or for evil.

For the sake of convenience, the number of times action is taken on something heard – true or false – is given below.

Leonato is informed by Antonio that a man of his has overheard Don Pedro tell Claudio that he is in love with Hero. Unintentionally false. (I,2)

Don John is informed by Borachio that he has overheard Don Pedro agree to woo Hero for himself and then hand her over to Claudio. True in essentials; Don Pedro, however, is to woo in Claudio's name. (I,3)

Don Pedro woos Hero, pretending to be Claudio. Half-false, with good intention. He is not Claudio, but it is Claudio who is in love with Hero. (II,1)

At the masked dance Benedick angers Beatrice (II,1) by reporting to her a conversation that he has invented. Here, however, it leads to no action by Beatrice, only retaliation in kind.

Don John tells Claudio that Don Pedro woos for himself. False, to make mischief.

Benedick confirms the news. False, though apparently Benedick believes it to be true.

Don Pedro, Claudio and Leonato arrange for Benedick to overhear them say how much Beatrice loves him. False, with good motive. (II,3)

Similarly Beatrice is brought to overhear Hero and Ursula say how much Benedick loves her. False, with good motive. (III,1.)

Don John tells Claudio that Hero is disloyal. False, with evil intent. (III,2)

The Watch overhear Borachio boast to Conrade how Claudio and

Don Pedro had been taken to see him woo Margaret impersonating Hero. True. (III,3)

It is reported that Hero is dead. False, with good motive. (IV,1)

Leonato tells Claudio to be ready to marry his 'niece'. False, with good motive. (V,1)

It will be seen from this how much in the play depends on falsehoods, told or designed to be overheard – both in the serious and the comic plot, and how much upon words overheard by chance. The criminal had relied on convincing his victims by planning that they should overhear a pre-arranged conversation. His scheming is brought to light by the Watch's overhearing an unguarded conversation.

Atmosphere

The central situation in *Much Ado about Nothing* is similar to that in *Cymbeline* (one of the later plays) – a woman is unjustly slandered and her lover rejects her. There is a confession in both, and things are cleared up by accident in both. Practically every character in both is deceitful at some point. Both have a tragic atmosphere, although a tragic ending is avoided. In the later play things are righted not so much from within as from a divine intervention from without: in *Much Ado about Nothing*, however, they come right by virtue of a certain sanative power in human nature, particularly in the youth of the play. In the one we are prepared for the worst, and in the other have good hope for the best. We wonder in the one that it could have ended well, and see in the other that it must have done.

On Hero's wedding morning there is an atmosphere of tragedy. She feels a sense of impending disaster in the air, a foreboding and nameless dread that makes her mistrust a happy day. The dramatic reason for this is to create suspense: Hero's nerves are on edge, and this is communicated to the audience – they feel that something dreadful is going to happen and yet do not know what, and this in turn heightens their attention.

While the play has tragedy, it has not the drive and energy of some plays, for example, *Romeo and Juliet*, *Julius Caesar* or *The Merchant of Venice*.

In *Much Ado about Nothing* the tragic foreboding is skilfully lightened by comic relief. The play opens with festivity and revelry, and it has a sparkle of bubbling gaiety. This is because Benedick and Beatrice make a more powerful impression than Hero and Claudio, and our sympathies are mainly absorbed in them. Then there is the self-important bumbledom of the Watch. Shakespeare has a keen eye for a genuinely comic or ludicrous figure or situation. In addition to the sheer fun there is a grip of character which increases the value of the play as a painting of life. Shakespeare's art is not bound down by the technical divisions of the schools; he strives to create a form for himself in which he may represent neither comedy nor tragedy alone, but human life.

Together in one play we have tragic power, deep feeling, rare beauty, sportive gaiety and happy romance. Shakespeare depicts life, bending one way or the other as he will, like a piece of shot silk in different lights. Sunshine and shadow are never very far away from one another, and sometimes we find it hard to distinguish where one ends and the other begins.

Setting

The great majority of Shakespeare's plays, apart from the English histories, are set in places abroad, a device which of itself gave them a romantic colouring. The local colour, however, is that of Elizabethan England, whether the story is one of Italy, Egypt or Denmark, and in whatever age (see p.7). At that time, for playwright and audience alike, the life and spirit of a play mattered more than strict accuracy in local colour. People saw in the drama a reflection of their own life and experiences; its appeal was not analytical or educational, but human.

Further, in those days people were untravelled and uneducated, and anachronisms would not strike a false note in an age more familiar with stories than with their settings. Though *Much Ado about Nothing* takes place nominally in Messina, we are never very far from the England Shakespeare knew.

Above all, there is the 'Watch' (a term for the police officers of the day). They were a sort of civil Home Guard, who did a job by day and took turns of duty in the 'Watch' at night, or in case of emergency. Shakespeare makes their muddle-headed zeal a subject of satire in his plays, as he portrays their officious self-importance when free to act in a capacity which gives them authority over their fellows. On official occasions (e.g. IV,2) they were entitled to 'gowns' of office.

In London circles Shakespeare would doubtless have been invited to an after-supper mask (masked dance). This kind of social evening was very popular at the time *Much Ado* was written and had not yet developed into the more ambitious and aristocratic entertainment it became later in Shakespeare's life under the patronage of James I.

Musicians are apparently classed as 'attendants' (I,2,). In those days musicians ranked low in public esteem, and a great lord paid his cook more than he paid his chief musician. Since ballads were now printed on broadsheets and were not the monopoly of professional minstrels, ballad-makers (mentioned scornfully by Benedick in I,1) ranked even lower. Three dances mentioned (in conversation) are 'a Scotch jig' (in Italy!), 'a measure' and 'a cinque pace', all of them well-known Elizabethan dances. Elizabethan court dances were elaborated from folk dances, such as a Scotch jig, and both kinds of dancing were popular on the public stage.

Leonato's household and his relations with the Watch stamp him as the Lord of the Manor of Shakespeare's day.

On the wedding morning the bridegroom (accompanied by 'all the gallants of the town') goes very early to the bride's house to take her to church for the ceremony, as was the Elizabethan custom.

Don Pedro refers to a 'dumb-show' (II,3). In pre-Shakespearian drama the 'dumb-show' was the plot of a play acted briefly without words before the beginning of the play proper.

A 'pleached bower' gives an Italian flavour to Leonato's garden, but not for long, for we find that it is a bower of English 'honeysuckle', that the habits of lapwings and hawks are familiar, that trout are caught by 'tickling' and birds by bird-lime.

Some of the more cruel pastimes of the age are represented. When a 'bear-ward' was mentioned (II,1) most of the audience would immediately think of the performing bears at a bear-pit in the vicinity of the Globe Theatre. Elsewhere (I,1) Benedick refers to archery practice at a cat 'in a bottle'.

And so one could go on, from usurers' chains in town to thistles and drizzling rain in the country, but more important than specific allusions is the English flavour throughout.

Structure and style

Structure

There are two main plots and two sub-plots in *Much Ado about Nothing*.

Main plots

1 The Hero–Claudio plot. Serious, with characters of noble birth.
2 The Beatrice–Benedick plot. Comic, with characters of noble birth.

Sub-plots

1 The Margaret–Borachio plot. Serious, with characters of low birth.
2 The Dogberry and Verges episodes. Comic, with characters of low birth.

A play with four separate elements might easily become confused, but these four elements are interwoven with consummate skill.

Contrast is a fundamental principle of Shakespearian drama. The comic and the serious jostle one another through this play (as they do in life), with Shakespeare heightening comic and serious scenes by juxtaposition. The student should notice the disposition of the scenes of the serious Hero–Claudio plot and the comic Beatrice–Benedick plot. And so between the parallel pairs of lovers: Claudio is trapped into thinking Hero false, Benedick and Beatrice are trapped into thinking each other truly devoted. Without Margaret and Borachio's part the climax of the main serious plot could never have happened; without the Watch it could never have been shown to be based on a lie. The irony is supreme. Those who try to deceive Benedick and Beatrice at the same time are being deceived themselves. Those who try to separate Hero and Claudio in so doing join Benedick and Beatrice. The climax of the serious plot (the denunciation of Hero) leads in the same scene to the climax of the comic plot (the admission by the two who had scorned love that they are in love).

The Watch hear of Borachio's villainy and arrest him as soon as it has been carried out, and this lessens the sense of tragedy, for, even at the time of Claudio's repudiation of Hero, the audience knows that the deception will soon be found out and the evil righted (or, in technical terms, the dramatic solution provided).

The different strands are thus firmly dovetailed together, otherwise the play would be 'broken-backed' and fall apart into two separate plays.

Style

Professor Edward Dowden (1843–1913) author of several books on Shakespeare gives an excellent summary of the development of Shakespeare's style.

> In the earliest plays the language is sometimes as it were a dress put upon the thought – a dress ornamented with superfluous care; the idea is at times hardly sufficient to fill out the language in which it is put; in the middle of plays (*Julius Caesar* serves as an example) there seems a perfect balance and equality between the thought and its expression. In the latest plays this balance is disturbed by the preponderance or excess of the ideas over the means of giving them utterance. The sentences are close-packed; there are 'rapid and abrupt turnings of thought, so quick that language can hardly follow fast enough; impatient activity of intellect and fancy, which having once disclosed an idea, cannot wait to work it orderly out'; 'the language is sometimes alive with imagery'.

Much Ado is Shakespeare in his middle years. The poetry is not so beautiful as that of the great Shakespearian plays, but, as everywhere in Shakespeare, graphic and figurative language abounds, and the vividness and variety of the imagery is to be noted. There are not as many expressions in *Much Ado* which have 'caught on' and become proverbial as there are in some plays. One, however, is 'The fashion wears out more apparel than the man' (III,3), and another,

> For there was never yet philosopher
> That could endure the toothache patiently. (V,1,35–6)

The normal line in Shakespeare's plays is a blank verse iambic pentameter. There is much variation however, making the verse more interesting to listen to and the dialogue more adapted to different characters. The songs or lyrics are, of course, in rhyme and differ in metre also.

Only one quarter of *Much Ado* is in verse; prose predominates owing to the large number of humorous scenes. There is only one play of Shakespeare's with more prose proportionately, and that is *The Merry Wives of Windsor.* The two nearest *Much Ado* are two other romantic comedies, *As You Like It* and *Twelfth Night.* It is interesting, therefore, to note that these four plays all belong to the same period of Shakespeare's life and were all written between late 1598 and 1601.

When prose is used in Shakespeare's plays it is with set intent. Prose is invariably the language of comic characters and characters of lower social position, such as Dogberry and Verges. This was a literary convention at a time when literature was aristocratic and the chief characters in plays (as in life) were kings and nobles. Scenes in which the lower orders of society figure are a contrast; these people are shown as living on a lower plane of feeling than the main characters and the contrast in the medium of expression – prose instead of verse – is in perfect keeping. It follows that there is more prose in the comedies. Sharpness of repartee, on which so much of *Much Ado* depends, would be impossible in verse. Hence we find prose the medium for the witty dialogue of the play.

The changes from prose to verse and verse to prose in the various scenes of *Much Ado* should be carefully studied and the reasons for them sought. Act I,1 is in prose until Claudio and Don Pedro are left alone and Claudio is stirred to speak of his love to someone who will listen to him seriously. Don John's surly nature is ill-suited to the beauty of verse (I,3). The only speech in Act II,1 in verse is where Claudio is emotionally moved thinking that he has lost Hero. When, in Scene 3, the talk is of music, verse naturally harmonizes with the subject. Benedick's line towards the end of the scene ('Fair Beatrice, I thank you for your pains') may be a blank verse line, a fitting expression of his new-found emotion.

At first sight it may appear strange that Act III,1 is in

verse, while Act III,3 (the corresponding trick on Benedick) is in prose. This may be to differentiate the women's part from the men's, and also perhaps because the women talk in more tender and less flippant fashion than the men. Beatrice's speech when the other two have gone is at the emotional level of verse, and is further differentiated by being in rhyming verse. The wedding scene preliminaries are in prose, but when emotion is roused the language passes naturally into verse. While everybody is overwrought it remains in verse. Even Benedick and Beatrice speak in verse here, emphasizing their noble natures. But when they stay behind on their own they slip unobtrusively into prose.

In Act V,1 the language of people who 'wring under the load of sorrow' is verse, until Benedick (bringing a touch of comedy) comes in, and, of course, later on Dogberry and Verges. When Leonato's heart is full of righteous anger his speech rises to verse. Even Borachio speaks in verse at a time like this when he is deeply moved. Dogberry, of course, is too earthy for verse, and Leonato bids him farewell in prose while he has verse for everyone else. Rhyming verse fits Scene 3, as the whole scene is in the nature of a chant or ritual. The preliminaries of the happy marriage ceremony are in verse; even Benedick and Beatrice speak in verse here, until their wit gets the better of them, and they speak as they have always done.

In a good play the style naturally reflects the character of the person speaking. Contrast the short, churlish sentences of Don John, e.g. in I,3 or III,2, or in verse in IV,1, with the long, deliberate, steady sentences of the Friar. Similarly with the imagery. A soldier's similes and metaphors come naturally to Benedick – 'I stood like a man at a mark, with a whole army shooting at me. She speaks poniards, and every word stabs'; 'like an honest man and a soldier'; 'these paper bullets of the brain': whereas the Friar takes his illustrations from the fire that burns men's errors (IV,1,161–66), and Hero from the life of the court (III,1,9–11). Sometimes the similes have a rare beauty, one (spoken by a woman) being

The pleasant'st angling is to see the fish
Cut with her golden oars the silver stream,
And greedily devour the treacherous bait.

The beauty of another serves to stand out against something foul.

You seem to me as Dian in her orb,
As chaste as is the bud ere it be blown;
But you are more intemperate in your blood
Than Venus, or those pamper'd animals
That rage in savage sensuality.

The use Shakespeare makes of contrast in larger measure in the construction of his play has already been mentioned. It should also be noticed in the phrasing of single lines (antithesis). e.g. 'Doing, in the figure of a lamb, the feats of a lion'; 'A kind overflow of kindness. . . . How much better is it to weep at joy than to joy at weeping.'

The student will also notice the antithesis of 'golden' and 'silver' in the quotation above. The antithetical form of much of the dialogue of the play was the fashion at the time that *Much Ado* was written. There are fashions in literary style as in everything else. This fashion of speech and writing was set off by John Lyly's *Euphues* (1579) and was known as 'Euphuism'. It is usually alliterative as well, as in the first example above. The whole of Act I,3 is in this euphuistic style. The verbal combats of Benedick and Beatrice are in the same style, as in Beatrice's reply to Benedick's thanks at the end of Act II, in which she takes up two of his words and tosses them about. 'I took no more pains for those thanks than you take pains to thank me: if it had been painful, I would not have come.'

Alliteration is used for emphasis other than that of euphuistic antithesis, of course, e.g. 'O, what authority and show of truth/Can cunning sin cover itself withal!'

Leonato's sorrow in his only child is emphasized by repetition.

I might have said 'No part of it is mine;
This shame derives itself from unknown loins'?
But mine and mine I loved and mine I praised
And mine that I was proud on, mine so much
That I myself was to myself not mine,
Valuing of her.

In Elizabethan times punning was extremely popular, and this kind of verbal trickery (what the Elizabethans would call 'conceits') is prevalent in Shakespeare's earlier plays. Punning is second nature to nearly every character in *Much Ado about Nothing*. The double meaning is generally quite obvious; in cases of difficulty an explanation is given in the textual notes.

There occur in *Much Ado about Nothing* little circumstantial details (used sparingly, so as not to interfere with the main impression) which give a clearer definition to the picture. 'For she'll be up twenty times a night, and there will she sit in her smock till she have writ a sheet of paper.' For instance, here Beatrice could not have been in love with Benedick long, he had been back from the wars only a day or two, but the details supposedly stamped on Hero's mind give an impression of truth.

Notice, too, the use of sympathetic background. This is an old device, whereby the weather harmonizes with the events in the story or play to suit the atmosphere. So the happy scenes take place out of doors in fine weather, but Borachio declares his villainy to Conrade by night in a drizzle.

In considering the style of a play the student should remember that there is a difference between literary and dramatic prose – or verse for that matter. In a play the style must be natural and convincing when spoken at the speed and in the manner of conversation, and in *Much Ado* Shakespeare is a master of dramatic prose as of dramatic blank verse.

Characters

Hero

Is she not a modest young lady?

Hero is only the nominal heroine of *Much Ado*. She naturally takes second place to Beatrice when they are together. She is more acted upon than acting. Hence the effect of the gross wrong done her is pitiful rather than tragic. Hero does not bring it upon herself by her own character. A certain pathos clings round her; she is at the mercy of outside forces: a beautiful and virtuous lady is to be sacrificed for somebody else's revenge on her betrothed, and he lacks faith enough in her to defend her.

Hero is gentle, patient and self-possessed, and shows none of Claudio's panicky whims. She is not so highly strung as Beatrice. She follows where others lead and shows little initiative. She is an obedient daughter. She accepts her father's directions as to how she shall treat one lover, and before long calmly agrees to transfer to another. When her father enjoins her, 'Daughter, remember what I told you: if the prince do solicit you in that kind, you know your answer', Hero replies not a word – such a one as Coriolanus calls a 'gracious silence'. Leaving out of account Act III,1, she speaks fewer than fifty lines in the play.

Hero is the archetype governor's daughter, content to woo through the proper channels. The rights of daughters in those days were not so clearly defined or exercised. After Claudio has publicly thrown her off on a false charge, Hero agrees to be put out of the way 'dead' for as long as may be, and then to go to marriage as somebody else. One can just imagine Beatrice's reactions to such a procedure! Her charm and tenderness are negative: they consist in falling in with whatever arrangement will make things work smoothly, in not making herself awkward. Her stature suits her disposition; she is 'Leonato's short daughter' – not so likely to be noticed as her taller cousin.

When dealing with her women-folk, however, about more trifling day-to-day matters, Hero can make up her mind for herself and stick to it – 'I'll wear none but this'. She enters with good will into the trick played on Beatrice and acts her part well. She is even sportive in this scene, and may not naturally be so quiet as she is when in the presence of Beatrice. In this connection, however, it was hardly the thing for her to steal one of Beatrice's letters from her pocket and make its contents known, even if only in fun.

Not once does Hero utter an unkind word to anybody, not even to Claudio when he disgraces her. We might think that an outburst here would be a natural sign of her innocence. But Shakespeare knew better. To say little when wrongly accused is a sign of her sincerity and truth. Sincere natures are not noisy and declamatory. Unreal feeling instinctively tries to disguise itself in words – the more we feel, the less we speak usually. Hero denies Claudio's charge in eight monosyllables – 'I talk'd with no man at that hour, my lord.' At the second wedding ceremony she unmasks herself, and again without flourish and all but the simplest words.

And when I lived, I was your other wife:
And when you loved, you were my other husband.

Finally, Hero's unembittered acceptance of the man who had so little confidence in her that he could do her a great wrong in public shows generous forgiveness. Whether this is goodness or weakness the student must decide for himself. Her love is a dutiful love. She does not come to Claudio with rejoicing. It is a social arrangement. She loves him as much as she would any other man whom her father considered a suitable match. At first she is prepared to marry Don Pedro, and then accepts Claudio.

This is another reason why the tragedy of *Much Ado* is not the tragedy of a breaking heart. Hero is not necessarily insincere: she may well have trusted her father's judgement better than her own, as it would appear girls more commonly did in Shakespeare's day. Such a nature is happier leaning on someone else and feels nervous without support. Her marriage probably stood more chance of turning out happily than one consumed by passion at the outset, like that of Romeo and Juliet. Hero would take pleasure in carrying out the daily humdrum duties that come to every marriage – even those of the nobility – and she would not be likely to quarrel with her husband, for she would be glad for him to make the decisions.

One of the most praiseworthy qualities about Hero is that she betrays no trace of jealousy that Beatrice gets more attention than she, in fact she probably prefers it that way, and may even be said to be proud of her. She is one of those who are happier in the background away from people's notice. Hero seldom speaks unless spoken to, and not always then. Were she made a strong or resolute character, or a talkative one, she would cease to be the foil to Beatrice that Shakespeare intended her to be.

In common with all Shakespeare's heroines (save Juliet, whose mother is against her) Hero is motherless. The dramatic effect of this is to throw them on their own resources in moments of stress – they have no other woman on whom they can rely, and this awakens our sympathy for their lonely hand and increases the pathos of their situation. In Hero's case, however, the pathos is less absolute, for Beatrice never wavers in her support, though her understanding has not the tenderness of that of a mother for her child.

Claudio

I know not how to pray your patience

It is difficult to reconcile the 'young Florentine's' repute on the battlefield with his lack of manliness in the play. He certainly does not seem to be of the stuff of which heroes are made.

Claudio's first words concern Hero, and she is seldom out of his conversation in the first scene. However, his love misses the intensity of Romeo's, for instance. He is tremendously wrapped up in himself, and we feel no attraction for this highly self-conscious lover. His is a sentimental sort of love. Claudio plays with the idea of considering himself in love and tries what it is like. His love for Hero is in his fancy rather than his heart. He cannot help talking about it. He is very fond of the sound of his own voice. Being a little nervous, Claudio gets Don Pedro to do his courting for him. When he comes to marry Hero he has not spoken to her. It is doubtful whether real love would make this approach or could keep this distance. His love is a pose: he loves no one better than himself.

Claudio trusts little. In the course of his wooing of Hero by proxy he takes the word of a quondam enemy against a prince for whom he had been proud to fight. And when he believes Don Pedro to have won Hero for himself, Claudio just accepts the situation – 'Farewell, therefore, Hero.' One would expect a man really in love to have done his own wooing. The purpose of his distrust of Don Pedro in the construction of the play is to make his acceptance of Don John's word against Hero more credible. Future events thus cast their shadows before, and we are more inclined to accept the improbability when it occurs. Our belief is forewarned, so to speak.

On the other hand, having found out Don John with a false tale once, it was ordinary prudence for Claudio to suspect a second tale coming from the same source. He has no common sense. Perhaps one reason why his youth is emphasized is to bring home his lack of experience of life – 'boy', 'a very forward March-chick', 'that young start-up', 'My Lord Lackbeard'.

Claudio appears to believe Don John's more serious story out of self-righteous indignation. His pride is wounded at the idea that a woman who had the honour to be betrothed to him should play him false. Beatrice can see through him when she says that he is 'civil as an orange, and something of that jealous complexion', and later, 'Count Comfect; a sweet gallant', adding, 'but men are only turned into tongue'. In his self-conceit Claudio thinks more of the wrong done to him than the shame to Hero. He makes no allowances, for he looks at it only from his own point of view. A kind and generous man would have gone to her quietly to talk it over. He allows for no possible explanation. Instead he jumps to conclusions and resolves on a cruel method of showing her up.

Even if his accusation were true the scene in the church would be more of a disgrace to him than to her. 'A princely testimony' is Beatrice's derisive comment. Had he any thought for her he would have wanted the matter hushed up. He puts his own wounded pride above her feelings. Claudio's action in church is not the result of a sudden outburst of temper: it is a deliberately calculated plan, determined on the previous night, and before there is any proof of Hero's guilt. Further his vengeance is directed at the daughter of his host, in whose house he has been well received;

a scene in the church at his daughter's wedding must upset Leonato.

Claudio's idea of his own self-importance blinds him to all other considerations. His whole performance in the church is over-stilted, for effect before an audience. In the denunciation scene, before Hero faints he speaks at length. When Hero is vindicated and Leonato trounces Claudio in sarcastic words, 'I know not how to pray your patience', says Claudio, 'yet I must speak'. He is not too much put out by Hero's disloyalty and death to joke the next morning in light-hearted fashion – 'We are high-proof melancholy and would fain have it beaten away'. 'Sir, your wit ambles well', says Benedick, 'it goes easily'. Claudio's jest about Leonato and Antonio, when they are upset at the charge against Hero and have challenged him, is unkindly in tone. 'We had like to have had our two noses snapped off with two old men without teeth.' It is to be said to his credit, however, that while Claudio does not accept the challenge of two old men he accepts that of Benedick, who is nearer his own age.

After Hero's innocence is proved he can see no fault in 'poor Claudio' – 'Yet sinn'd I not but in mistaking.' At the end of his tirade against Hero in the church he had vowed

For thee I'll lock up all the gates of love,
And on my eyelids shall conjecture hang,
To turn all beauty into thoughts of harm,
And never shall it more be gracious.

But he soon forgets this when Leonato's 'over-kindness' produces another lady for him to marry. His penance is as theatrical as his denunciation. Claudio talks of Hero's 'fame which never dies', but it has died in his heart before he has left the monument after doing his 'rite' (a 'rite' only, it is to be feared). One girl is as good as another; let bygones be bygones, and he will have another try in the morning. Claudio's words and actions are those of neither a deep nor a sincere nature, and we are perhaps least of all impressed when he is able so casually to transfer his affections to Hero's cousin. In fairness it must be remembered that Claudio is willing, if necessary, to take her as a penance, but he knows where his interest lies.

It should be noted that Hero's attraction for Claudio is not independent of her fortune. 'Hath Leonato any son, my lord?' (I,1). That such a question should be put makes one wonder whether, if the answer had been 'Yes', Hero would have held the same favour in his eyes. Does Leonato recognize a rapacious streak in his make-up when he recommends his 'niece' to Claudio with the information that 'she alone is heir to both of us' (V,1,303)?

We cannot help feeling sorry that, after what he had made her suffer, Hero could still want to marry him as he comes jauntily to marry another. Claudio is quite unworthy of her, and it seems a pity that she will have to put up with such a man. For his part, Claudio gets more, much more, than he deserves.

Beatrice and Benedick

By my troth, a pleasant-spirited lady

In despite of his quick wit . . . he shall fall in love with Beatrice

These two are inseparable and cannot sensibly be discussed in isolation. The alliteration in their names is no coincidence.

Much Ado is technically classed as a comedy because the lives of its hero and heroine are not sacrificed. (It would have been a tragedy if Hero had really died from shock.) Beatrice and Benedick go a long way towards investing the play with the spirit of comedy. We are more interested in them than we are in Hero and Claudio; and so is Shakespeare. They are hearty and lively, awake to the excitement of living; they do not walk about with the dreamy languor of a Claudio.

Benedick comes close to the Elizabethan ideal of a gentleman, a good 'all-rounder', soldier, courtier and scholar, 'of a noble strain, of approved valour and confirmed honesty'. He is more a man of action than a scholar, it is true, but at least he is fond of reading in his spare time and has some knowledge of the classics. Music affords him little pleasure – 'Is it not strange that sheep's guts should hale souls out of men's bodies?' Nevertheless, one of the qualifications for his ideal wife is for her to be 'an excellent musician': perhaps he has it in the back of his mind that she should grace the home with social accomplishment. With regard to his honesty, it has to be admitted that it is not confirmed enough to prevent his listening to a private conversation between two of his friends. The same can be said of Beatrice, but in her case she has been told that Hero and Ursula were talking about her and the temptation was therefore stronger.

Both Beatrice and Benedick fancy themselves as wits and in 'a kind of merry war' turn everything to jest, especially one another. 'They never meet but there's a skirmish of wit between them.' The chief subject of their witticisms is marriage; and so much have they traduced it in jest that they cannot support it in truth – 'Well, if ever thou dost fall from this faith, thou wilt prove a notable argument.' Their wit is intellectual, brilliant and sparkling, even if a trifle self-conscious. Their conversation is an unending sequence of puns and antithesis. They pride themselves on their wit, and for that reason try to vanquish each other in a 'skirmish of wit' every time they meet. They are intensely annoyed that their wit should be considered to be 'out of the "Hundred Merry Tales"' or like that of 'the prince's jester'. Like Claudio they are always talking – 'evermore tattling'. But Beatrice and Benedick are more witty and have more good sense than Claudio, so we do not tire of their conversation so soon.

Beatrice has the outlook of the modern emancipated woman: she is as good as any man, and 'would it not grieve a woman to be overmastered with a piece of valiant dust?' She would not have a man chosen for her by someone else – 'Yes, faith; it is my cousin's duty to make curtsy and say, "Father, as it pleases you". But yet for all that, cousin, let him be a handsome fellow, or else make another curtsy and say, "Father, as it please me"' – as she would have done. Beatrice will carve out her own fortune, as, indeed, she does (notwithstanding that it was under a misapprehension).

The way the marriage of Beatrice and Benedick is contrived is the great joke of *Much Ado*, and is the cause of much fun; for instance, when Beatrice is sent to Benedick just after he has heard of her supposed love for him, and he says, 'Here comes Beatrice. By this day! she's a fair lady: I do spy some marks of love in her.' Or when, having laughed at Claudio's careful attention to dress since he fell in love, he shaves off his beard (had he heard that she 'could not endure a husband with a beard on his face'?), or puts his discomfiture down to toothache and she hers to a cold. And especially when Benedick strides forth in all seriousness to challenge his late friend Claudio as a means of winning his lady's favour.

Now they are fallen 'from this faith', as prophesied they prove 'a notable argument', and it is their turn to be satirized. Benedick had vowed that 'the sensible Benedick' would never bear 'the yoke' of marriage). The irony of it is that he should marry the woman who had sworn, 'No, uncle, I'll none' (i.e. no husband)! Claudio would scarce trust himself not to turn husband, 'though I had sworn the contrary'. Beatrice and Benedick take each other to be husband and wife having sworn the contrary. Indeed at the end of the play, Benedick is counselling someone else to get married!

More important than the wit of Benedick and Beatrice are their good sense, and their kind and loyal natures. After Hero's denunciation Beatrice is the first to say, 'O, on my soul, my cousin is belied!' She has no reasons for saying so, she just knows it. Her assurance speaks for itself. Benedick is the first to realize that 'The practice of it lives in John the bastard'. Their common sympathy with a woman wronged brings them more closely together.

Benedick Surely I do believe your fair cousin is wronged.
Beatrice Ah, how much might the man deserve of me that would right her!

Beatrice realizes that she needs a man to turn to for help. 'O that I were a man for his [Claudio's] sake! or that I had any friend would be a man for my sake!' Benedick's sympathy for Hero is sincere, and not an affectation to stand him in good stead with Beatrice. He passes Beatrice's test to prove his love and goes out to risk his life. He is pale when he delivers his challenge to a former friend, the last person in the world he expected to fight. It evidently cost him something. Claudio finds him in no mood for jest. Benedick's parting from Don Pedro shows his 'noble strain': it is courteous, dignified and restrained, yet unmistakably firm, without a trace of Claudio-like declamation.

Benedick assured Margaret that his wit was a 'most manly wit' that would not 'hurt a woman'. His wit will not hurt a woman and his sword will fight for a woman's reputation. We can believe that he is a brave soldier, with the knightly chivalry of which Claudio was so conspicuously destitute. Benedick is a strong masculine character, and Claudio a weak one. Benedick's concern for Hero's future is significant when, just before his marriage, he tells Claudio to 'love my cousin'. Benedick and Beatrice are not just empty chatterboxes, proof against everything serious, they have an earnest side when occasion offers.

When he comes off worse in a bout of wit with Beatrice, it may seem to Benedick that she 'speaks poniards, and every word stabs'. But Beatrice, like Benedick, is both kind and considerate. At the beginning of the play when she sees that her talk of Benedick is not understood by the Messenger and is making one of lower rank feel uncomfortable, she at once finishes the conversation and tries to put him at his ease – 'Do, good friend.' When her uncle hints that she has been talking too long, Beatrice courteously withdraws, and shows no ill-feeling (II,2).

If only they had the sense to realize it, these two were made for one another. Their wit, their intelligence, their disposition, their interest in each other (from the start they are never out of one another's thoughts), their whole personality make them admirably suited. The very fact that they so often said they would not get married showed that marriage was in their minds, even if in a negative sense. They protest too much. The 'conspirators' make possible a natural alliance that is prevented by a barrier of false pride and mock obstinacy. Benedick is sensible enough to admit it, and in an incomparably humorous vein easily passes off his change of face. 'When I said I would die a bachelor, I did not think I should live till I were married.' The real reason, of course, is that until now he has not met the woman who could stir his affection and respect. He has thus assumed the façade of a woman-hater.

Beatrice has had plenty of opportunities to get married, but has found none of her wooers suitable and has mocked them all 'out of suit'. But all the time Benedick and Beatrice had an underlying interest in and respect for one another. Their delight in their verbal combats is significant. When Benedick went to the wars he had made a big impression on Beatrice. When he comes back and talks to her father without noticing her she draws his attention to herself. Before ever Benedick was conscious of any affection he had thought that Beatrice exceeded Hero 'as much in beauty as the first of May doth the last of December'. When Hero swoons and Beatrice acts impulsively in an emergency, Benedick is the first man upon whom she calls for help, apart from Hero's father. She evidently feels intuitively that he is a man to be relied on. The man who is not afraid to bear his sword against Claudio has moral courage too, and is not going to be put off by what people say about him. 'Dost thou think I care for a satire or an epigram?'

Verbal wit of the type in which Beatrice and Benedick indulge was very popular in Shakespeare's day. We like it in small doses and tire of it sooner than Shakespeare's audiences would have done, but even so Shakespeare is careful not to overdo it and ennui is avoided as the lightning wit of these two fades in the second half of the play. So are the style and construction of the play bound up with the characters.

The home of Hero and Claudio would be a comfortable, conventional and dull sort of home, with Hero looking up to her lord and master, not wishing to cross him – or fearing his outbursts if she did. The home of Beatrice and Benedick would be bright and cheery, have vitality and energy, life in it would be exciting and husband and wife would be aware of things. They would not see eye to eye, but would face their differences together and work out a compromise in a not too serious give and take spirit. Beatrice would be a person, not a shadow; she would keep her independence, and it must be remembered that loyalty and independence may march side by side. A woman who values her independence is usually loyal to the man who gives it her.

The interplay of various motives in Benedick and Beatrice sometimes leaves their actions open to more than one interpretation. They are more human because they are wider than any single interpretation of their characters. How many times in life do we find an action interpreted differently by different people? This difference in approach does not cease when we come to judge people in plays or books.

In the structure of the play Beatrice and Benedick provide comic relief of a witty and intelligent kind (instead of a 'low' kind like that of Dogberry and Verges). They whip up the pace of the play. They provide character contrast with Hero and Claudio, and their romance is an ironic inversion of the main one.

A comparison of the way Benedick and Beatrice are tricked into thinking each other in love may help in the study of the play.

Benedick (II,3)	**Beatrice** (III,1)
The three actors express their surprise that Beatrice should be in love with Benedick.	Ursula expresses her surprise that Benedick should be in love with Beatrice.
Perhaps she counterfeits.	
No, her love, is obviously sincere. Further, there is an independent witness (Hero).	Independent witnesses – 'the prince and my new-trothed lord'.
She swears that she will not tell Benedick of it – he would scorn her.	'Rather I will go to Benedick And counsel him to fight against his passion.'
'I pray you, tell Benedick of it.' No – he would 'make but a sport of it and torment the poor lady worse'.	Hero has been asked to tell her of Benedick's love. No – she will 'make sport of it' (the identical words).
Praise of Beatrice; sweet, virtuous and wise – 'in everything but in loving Benedick'.	Praise of Benedick.
They praise Benedick, but say that on the whole 'he is unworthy so good a lady'.	Beatrice is too disdainful. She 'turns every man the wrong side out'.
Benedick comes out of hiding – 'This can be no trick': in short, staccato sentences (emphasizing his amazement) he resolves to put his detractions 'to mending' and return the affection of such a fair and virtuous lady as Beatrice.	Beatrice comes out of hiding – 'Can this be true?': in short sentences (but not so jerky as Benedick's, as they are in verse) she resolves to give up her 'contempt' and 'maiden pride', and return the affection of such a deserving man as Benedick.

Don John

I had rather be a canker in a hedge than a rose in his grace

Don John is the villain of the piece, an early sketch of Edmund in *King Lear*. His first words strike the keynote of his character: they are words of thanks, but they are blunt and rough and surly, though whether to the point of rudeness would depend entirely on how they were said. Bastardy makes him jealous of his half-brother, who comes as a matter of course into an inheritance from which his birth excludes him. Don John is embittered; society is against him through no fault of his own and his pride is hurt. Shakespeare's villains are not merely agents in a plot, their actions are related to their characters and circumstances.

He has tried to vindicate himself in open rebellion and has failed. Now he tries subtler means. Not, this time, against Don Pedro, but against his chief officer ('right hand'), who has gained praise and honour by his defeat. 'That young start-up hath all the glory of my overthrow.' Don John is ripe for any mischief and is unconcerned just what particular evil he sets his hand to. Before he knows who is to be married, he asks, 'Will it serve for any model to build mischief on?' (I,3), and when he knows that it is Claudio he is delighted. 'If I can cross him any way, I bless myself every way.' Any harm to Don Pedro or his associates will 'prove food to his displeasure'. That his spiteful malice dishonours a lady is merely incidental.

Don John smarts from a sense of inferiority. Having little standing among the guests of Leonato he associates with his followers; it brings more pleasure to his warped nature to be looked up to by inferiors than to mix as less than an equal with those more exalted. Don John likes to be someone who counts, if not in love then in hate.

Thus it satisfies his ego to imagine that he is of consequence, that he is in everybody's mind at the supper – 'Their cheer is the greater that I am subdued.' Although he says, 'Let us to the great supper', Don John apparently changes his mind, for nobody sees him there. It would appear that it is too much for him gracefully to accept the reconciliation so generously offered. His bitterness gnaws at his heart – 'Would the cook were of my mind!' His first words were surly, and it is surly not to accept the invitation to the supper.

He has a pass at Claudio by telling him that his brother, Don Pedro, has double-crossed him and wooed Hero for himself. His success in that may have encouraged him to try a more serious delusion. 'Only to despite them I will endeavour anything,' he snarls.

Don John must have congratulated himself on his success. Coincidence and chance work in his favour. But in turn coincidence and chance work to unmask him. The tongue of his agent is loosed by drink and Borachio gives his story away to an associate without knowing that zealous, if not very intelligent, constables are within hearing. And by the slow process of official enquiry his villainous plot comes to light. Then he tries to save his own skin and leaves his underlings to face the consequences. Whether he is given his deserts when he is captured is a question Shakespeare very wisely leaves open.

Dogberry and Verges

But, masters, remember that I am an ass

Dogberry and Verges are the clowns of the play, fools at the heart of great events. They are not complex characters. Shakespeare hits them off in a few quick strokes and the main outlines of their characters are thrown into relief.

Little people are so delighted to get authority that they use it officiously in a way that (so they think) shows their superiority to lesser men. When self-conceited people are idiots as well the effect is ludicrous. What an outrage to Dogberry it is when somebody calls him an ass! 'Dost thou not suspect [respect] my place? . . . I am a wise fellow, and, which is more, an officer, and, which is more, a householder, and, which is more, as pretty a piece of flesh as any is in Messina, and one that knows the law, go to; and a rich fellow enough, go to; and a fellow that hath had losses, and one that hath two gowns and every thing handsome about him.' When the Sexton points out to Dogberry that he does not know the law well enough to examine in the right way he pretends that he knew all along – 'Yea, marry, that's the eftest way.'

The incompetence of these two constables, combined with Leonato's delegation of duty when he is in a hurry, means that their news is delayed. The Sexton, a man of greater intelligence, realizes its importance and sees that Leonato is told at once. It is a matter of supreme irony that Don John's clever and villainous plot should be discovered by a pompous old ass – or his assistant constables.

Nevertheless, the way these bungling constables try to do their job, to the best of their ability, is worthy of respect, and there is no reason why Leonato should not mean what he says when he thanks them for their 'care and honest pains'.

'Neighbour Verges' is the butt to Dogberry – he asks the necessary questions to 'draw' him or echoes his remarks, but suggests nothing for himself except to tell the Watch what to do if they hear a child cry in the night. Comedians usually work in twos like this. Dogberry swells with pride at Verges' admiration, but checks Verges if he gets too independent and seems about to usurp his superior authority. He speaks of him with kindly condescension – 'A good old man, sir; he will be talking: as they say, When the age is in, the wit is out' – a description equally true of himself. They are both men of many words and few ideas. They try to show the importance of their office by decking out their conversation with long words, with the result that it becomes a hotch-potch of malapropisms. This sort of humour has to be kept within bounds, however, for it tires an audience sooner than the trenchant wit of Benedick and Beatrice, and Dogberry and Verges have only four short scenes.

Murder of the Queen's English never fails to raise a laugh on the stage. It is so in casual conversation 'below stairs', but a tang of irony is added to the humour when the malapropisms of fools bemuddle the course of enquiry into important events. The questioning of the two prisoners (IV,2) is a masterpiece.

The Watch was a stock subject of satire in Shakespeare's time, just as little educated mayors of lesser towns are today. We are meant to laugh at them, but none the less they are drawn with a loving touch. The satire is good-humoured, without ill-feeling or bitterness. We can laugh at Dogberry and Verges and their associates without taking them too seriously. But they take themselves very seriously and are quite unconscious of the humour they provide, which adds to the fun. Shakespeare's wide tolerance enables him to suffer fools gladly.

Leonato

This good old man

Leonato's house provides the meeting-place for all these different characters.

He is a kindly old soul who makes everybody welcome, including Don John, and tries to give them all a good time in the accepted way. He has provided a home for Beatrice: for how long we do not know, but if from childhood, she must have been a 'handful' to bring up! He can join in a bit of fun – 'My lord, I am for you, though it cost me ten nights' watchings.' In fact it is Leonato's taking part in the deception that makes it conclusive for Benedick – 'I should think this a gull, but that the white-bearded fellow speaks it.' He has a lively wit, as keen as Benedick's, and he can return Benedick's knocks with interest.

Don Pedro I think this is your daughter.
Leonato Her mother hath many times told me so.
Benedick Were you in doubt, sir, that you asked her?
Leonato Signior Benedick, no; for then you were a child.
Don Pedro You have it full, Benedick.

Leonato has the courtesy to apologize to a servant (I,2) and graces Dogberry with the friendly address of 'honest neighbour' (III,5). He has been accused of too easily delegating his duties to Dogberry and Verges. This is surely a hard and unfair criticism, for what father would not think he was justified in delegating his duties on the wedding-day of his only daughter? Leonato can hardly be blamed for not wishing to be late on such an occasion, especially through stopping to listen to a couple of prosy old yokels like Dogberry and Verges. He would have come in for much more blame had he been any later for the ceremony: as it is, his absence holds it up for a time. To take any other view is unreasonably to judge him, wise in the knowledge of subsequent events.

Our censure of him for placing his daughter with any convenient gentleman who wanted her is a judgement on his time rather than on Leonato himself. So far as he was concerned, to do well for his daughter meant giving her to a man able to keep her in the style to which she was accustomed: which man did not particularly matter. A materialistic outlook, but not necessarily insincere or hypocritical.

When Hero is accused he is in a dilemma. His love for her is unquestionable – 'Bring me a father that so loved his child' – and his faith in her, but are not Don Pedro and Claudio honourable men? At first he joins to accuse Hero on their testimony. For a time his judgement is numbed by the shock – 'I know not'. Then he plucks up heart at Benedick's suggestion that it may be a plot of Don John's and mortification turns to angry thoughts of revenge. The sudden revulsions of feeling at a time like this are very true to life. He agrees to the Friar's plan as much in despair as in hope – 'Being that I flow in grief, the smallest twine may lead me.' After the sudden shock has passed, faith re-asserts itself; clouds are still around, but his sure trust in Hero is seen rising clearer above them. 'My soul,' he says, 'doth tell me Hero is belied.' Leonato denies Claudio's accusation and, old man as he is, is ready to defend the reputation of his 'innocent child' with his sword against all comers.

When Don John's plot is revealed Leonato generously – some would say too generously – forgives Claudio, as Claudio himself acknowledges. 'O noble sire, your over-kindness doth wring tears from me!'

And at the end he shows no ill will when Benedick overrules him in his own house. He lets him have his own way, and the play ends with a dance.

His brother Antonio has little personality of his own and is simply a foil to show up Leonato. His breathless, heady words in Act V,1, contrast with Leonato's more deliberate revenge. It is ironical that he who had 'spoken patience' to Leonato with conventional platitudes should in a few minutes get so enraged that he himself has to be restrained.

In other places Antonio just echoes Leonato's words, e.g. II,1 and his last speech in V,1.

His sense of honour is not above encouraging his servants to eavesdrop, and he himself runs to pass on their confidences.

Minor characters

Borachio and Conrade are willing accomplices to Don John in 'building mischief'. Borachio 'whips him behind the arras' when an opportunity comes to hear somebody's secrets, of which use may possibly be made later on. However, in so doing he is in good company in this play. Both are trustworthy servants. 'You are both sure, and will assist me?' Don John asks them. 'To the death, my lord,' unflinchingly vouches Conrade, and Borachio in milder terms, 'We'll wait upon your lordship.'

At first Conrade counsels philosophic acceptance of the situation ('patient sufferance') until a good opportunity for revenge should present itself. Borachio is the more forceful in mischief. Without him Hero would never have been disgraced. It is he who suggests to Don John the plot to be 'the death of this marriage' and the means (II,2). Like the constables who arrest him, Borachio is proud of his office. His satisfaction in the office of Don John's right-hand man, and also in the easy money he has made, finds prompt expression as soon as he meets someone to whom he can talk – 'I will, like a true drunkard, utter all to thee' (the name Borachio means 'drunkard').

In Borachio's favour it must be said that when he is caught he admits his crime, and indeed his confession implies regret. More striking is the way he springs to Margaret's defence as soon as Leonato implicates Margaret with him.

No, by my soul, she was not!
Nor knew not what she did when she spoke to me,
But always hath been just and virtuous
In anything that I do know by her.

Borachio had more honour than his master. He is man enough to stand by the woman who had unwittingly helped him in crime, and he does not leave her to fend for herself when he is discovered, as Don John does his associates.

It is by such touches that Shakespeare shows his truth to human nature. Men are not all good or all bad. There is some good in the worst of us and some bad in the best of us. There is a strain of goodness and honour in a villain like Borachio.

Conrade and Borachio are not servants in the ordinary sense of the word. They are gentleman followers of Don John, and in the class-conscious society of Elizabethan England there was a vast difference. See how Conrade takes offence at Dogberry's manner of address and reminds him that he is 'a gentleman'.

Margaret and Ursula are the corresponding gentlewomen. They too, like Borachio and Conrade, are not classed as servants. They attend the mask with Leonato and the Prince and other lords, and the way Margaret teases Beatrice in III,4 would be insolence in a servant. Yet they would not be above accepting rewards for services, and Benedick hints at one for Margaret if she will help him 'to the speech of Beatrice' (V,2).

Margaret is the more forceful of the two. She is not present at the duping of Beatrice, however, where Ursula plays a pretty part. She fancies herself as a wit, and in Act III,4, takes the place of Beatrice (who is 'exceeding ill'). 'What pace is this that thy tongue keeps?' asks Beatrice, and Benedick acknowledges that her wit 'is as quick as the greyhound's mouth' (V.2).

The part Margaret plays off stage is more fraught with consequence than what she does on it. By impersonating Hero she works more havoc than she dreams. Even if she agreed to do so unwillingly, to satisfy Borachio, as appears 'in the true course of all the question', it seems improbable that a woman of average intelligence would not see the connection between her action and the accusation against Hero which followed. In any case it was a pointless disguise, and not one becoming a loyal gentlewoman. Even if Margaret was not 'pack'd in all this wrong', it is an understatement for Leonato to say that she was 'in some fault'.

The student should notice how all the important characters, except Don John and the Friar, are matched in pairs. Naturally Don John is not paired off – his arch-villainy must stand on its own, and the Friar, as a churchman, is aloof from human affairs.

Claudio and Don Pedro
Claudio and Hero
Benedick and Beatrice
Dogberry and Verges
Leonato and Antonio
Borachio and Conrade
Margaret and Ursula
Margaret and Borachio (though not on the stage)

Scene summaries, textual notes and revision questions

Act I

Scene 1

A messenger comes to Leonato, Governor of Messina, and announces that Don Pedro, Prince of Arragon, is about to pay him a call on his way home after an action (presumably the suppression of a rebellion led by his half-brother, Don John). Leonato's daughter Hero and his niece Beatrice are with him, and Beatrice enquires after a certain Signior Benedick in the army, with whom, it appears, she has engaged in much repartee in the past.

Thereupon Don Pedro arrives, accompanied by Don John, with whom he is now reconciled, Claudio, a young and valiant soldier, and Benedick. They are all invited to stay with Leonato for a month. Signior Benedick and Beatrice resume their witty retorts. Claudio confides his love of Hero to Benedick, who makes fun of him, and to Don Pedro, who undertakes to do what he can to further his suit, indeed, to do his wooing for him in his disguise.

The first part of this scene gives the situation. The letter and the messenger are merely dramatic contrivances to acquaint the audience with events in a natural manner as part of the play.

Notice how the interest of the audience is aroused in Claudio and Benedick before they enter, so that when they appear it is in response to a longing of the audience to see them. They thus make a greater impression.

With the entrance of Don Pedro and his friends all the main characters of the play are on the stage. The action proper begins with the repartee between Benedick and Beatrice, and Claudio's acknowledgement of his love for Hero, the two main strands of the plot.

Don Sir or Master.

this action Not specified, but presumably the action in which Don John's rebellion was suppressed.

sort Since the messenger is answering Leonato's question, 'How many gentlemen have you lost?', it might be assumed that 'sort' here means 'rank'. Leonato, however, appears to interpret it as 'kind', unless we take it to imply that he thinks the lives of common men of no account.

name i.e. title.

figure ... lion Notice how the antithesis is helped by the corresponding alliteration. Such antithesis was very popular in Elizabethan times and therefore frequently occurred on the stage. The student will readily find other examples in this first scene (as well as throughout the play).

bettered Surpassed.

He hath ... of it The uncle does not come in the play (and is not invited to his nephew's wedding), but such a remark serves to give breadth to the play.

modest Moderate.

badge of bitterness Explained by Leonato's next enquiry. The metaphor is from the servant's 'badge' on his livery, the sign of the house he served.

kind Natural (as with the noun – 'each after his kind'). Such plays on words as 'kind and 'kindness' were also very popular on the stage.

Mountanto A fencing term – the name of an upward thrust. Beatrice is referring to Benedick's thrusts in repartee.

sort The word here undoubtedly means 'rank'. See note above.

pleasant Amusing.

bills Posters, presumably announcing a challenge. The word still exists in the compound 'handbills'.

Cupid Roman god of love.

flight An arrow for use at long ranges.

subscribed Set down his name (literally underneath), signed.

bird-bolt An arrow with a flat head, used for short distance shooting of birds without damaging the plumage.

I promised ... killing Implying that he would not have killed any.

tax Censure.

meet Level, 'quits'.

stomach Punning on 'stomach (i.e. appetite) for the fight'. Beatrice's turning the conversation to food is probably a punning rejoinder to 'meet'.

man i.e. servant.

stuffed man i.e. puppet (stuffed with straw).

five wits Made five to match the five senses.

difference A metaphor from heraldry, where a 'difference' is a mark on a coat of arms to distinguish two members of the same family. In other words, the only difference between Benedick and his horse is that he knows how to keep himself warm.

faith Faithfulness.

block Mould for a hat.
books i.e. good books.
an If.
study i.e. where the books are kept, library.
squarer Brawler, hooligan.
presently Immediately – the literal meaning.
a' A corruption of 'he'.
I will . . . lady The messenger cannot understand Beatrice, but sees that she is determined and spirited, and indicates that he does not wish to quarrel with her on account of his championing of Benedick. As soon as Beatrice sees that she is making one of lower rank feel uncomfortable she at once changes her tone – 'Do, good friend'.
is approached 'Is' instead of 'has' because 'approached' is a verb of motion (as in French). Cf. in the next line, 'You are come'.
his Probably not a personification, but simply 'its'. 'His' was the old neuter possessive, as well as the masculine.
fathers herself i.e. is like her father.
his head i.e. a head as old as his.
still Always – the usual meaning in Elizabethan English.
marks Takes any notice of.
it The personification is not continued.
convert Change.
dear Great. In Elizabethan English the word 'dear' intensified the meaning – you could have a 'dear friend' or a 'dear enemy', e.g. 'my dearest foe' (*Hamlet*, 1,3,182).
blood Nature, temperament, inclination.
humour Disposition; much the same as 'blood'. Cf. the title of Ben Jonson's play *Every Man in his Humour*, i.e. according to his mood, temperament or disposition.
predestinate i.e. for which he would otherwise be predestined.
parrot-teacher i.e. you keep on saying the same old things.
i' In.
a jade's trick i.e. slipping its collar.
That . . . Leonato While the duel of wits has been going on between Beatrice and Benedick, Don Pedro and Leonato have been talking apart.
thou The Elizabethan convention in the use of 'thou' and 'you' is illustrated in the conversation between Claudio and Benedick. Claudio addresses Benedick as 'thou', and Benedick Claudio as 'you'. 'Thou' was a sign of familiarity (used by a master or mistress to servants and between close friends), 'you' was a formal address, used, for example, by

servant to master. Benedick is not inclined to get confidential in this talk of love and keeps his distance. Claudio seeks closer confidences.

too brown Fair hair was the vogue in Shakespeare's time, since the Queen had fair hair (actually sandy), and in her old age, at the time Shakespeare wrote his play, she wore a false head of golden hair. Notice the punning antithesis in 'too brown for a fair praise', balancing the other antithesis.

sad Serious (a common meaning in Shakespeare).

Jack i.e. fellow – usually contemptuously, Jack being a very common Christian name.

Cupid Cupid was represented as blind.

Vulcan Roman god of fire and cunning artificer in metals. Benedick, in effect, says, 'Are you serious, or are you playing with us, as you would be if you told us that blind Cupid was "a good hare-finder" and Vulcan "a rare carpenter"'.

to go in the song i.e. to be in the same key, in harmony with you, in the same frame of mind.

with suspicion i.e. of having horns under it; in other words, having a wife who is unfaithful.

Go to An expression of slight remonstrance; the modern equivalent (curiously enough) would be 'Come, come.'

print Mark.

sigh away Sundays i.e. as a married man, miserable at home.

the old tale A tale containing a criminal's denial.

fetch me in Trap me (into an admission of love). When Claudio sees that Don Pedro is serious, and not making fun of him as Benedick was, he is glad to own his love.

in the force of his will By sheer willpower.

recheat A blast on a hunting-horn to assemble the hounds. The usual reference to horns on the forehead (see note above on 'with suspicion') is intended.

winded Sounded. Cf. *John Peel*, 'The huntsman winds his horn.'

fine Conclusion (Lat. *finis*).

finer i.e. better dressed because he has no wife to provide for). For the popularity of puns on the Elizabethan stage, see 'Structure and style' p.27.

blind Cupid See note on 'Cupid', above.

argument Subject, example.

bottle Wicker cover for a bottle, basket. A cat in a basket was used for a target at archery.

Adam A stock name for an archer; perhaps after Adam Bell, a famous ballad outlaw.

try Prove, test.
'In time ... yoke' A line (not quite word perfect) from Kyd's *Spanish Tragedy*.
pluck off ... forehead The sign of a man whose wife was unfaithful. See note on 'with suspicion', above.
horn-mad Stark mad (originally of horned beasts).
spent all his quiver Those pierced by Cupid's golden arrows were smitten by love.
Venice A byword for gaiety.
earthquake i.e. it will take an earthquake to make me quake. Or perhaps he means that an earthquake will be just as likely.
matter Sense.
tuition Care.
From my house ... Benedick Benedick's farewell is finished as if in a letter.
guarded trimmed round the edges (as with braid).
slightly basted on neither Lightly attached either.
old ends i.e. accustomed endings to letters.
Dost thou affect her Are you fond of her (have you affection for her)?
onward i.e. out.
break with Break the news to.
to twist so fine a story Exactly the metaphor in 'to spin a yarn'.
complexion Looks, appearance.
salved Excused.
treatise Account (of its growth).
the necessity Just as much (or as long) as is necessary.
once In short, in a word, once for all.
unclasp A metaphor from opening a book. Old books with clasps to lock them can be seen in museums: in Shakespeare's day books were valuable things.

Scene 2

It appears that Claudio and Don Pedro have been overheard (though not at the end of the previous scene). But the eavesdropper Antonio has mixed things up, and tells Leonato that it is Don Pedro who is in love with Hero. Leonato sends word to Hero, so that she may be prepared.

my cousin, your son The word 'cousin' was used loosely of any relationship or friendship in Elizabethan England. In his last speech in this scene Leonato uses it in a pleasant way to attendants, apparently interchangeable with 'friend'. So today a man calls a boy 'son' without any suggestion of the actual relationship.

music Group of musicians.

they 'News' is, strictly speaking, plural, though now always treated as singular.

event Result.

thick-pleached Thickly interwoven. A beautiful word, conjuring up a picture in itself.

orchard Garden. In Scene 1 the Prince and Claudio were not in Antonio's orchard, though Shakespeare was seldom very particular about details like this.

man See note p.48.

discovered Revealed (literally uncovered).

accordant Agreeable.

top i.e. forelock. The idiom is an old one.

break with See note above.

wit i.e. sense.

cry you mercy i.e. beg your pardon.

Scene 3

Don John, moody and resentful ('their cheer is the greater that I am subdued'), has stayed away from the supper to which Leonato has invited his guests.

He hears another version of how Don Pedro plans to woo Hero for Claudio (again from an eavesdropper). He purposes mischief.

In this scene Don John's part as the villain is indicated. It is a scene full with possibilities for the future and awakens the suspense of the audience.

What the good-year A petty oath.

you Notice that Conrade addresses his master as 'you', but in reply is addressed as 'thou'. See note on 'thou', p.49.

sad See note p.50.

measure Moderation. Punning on the word used in Conrade's speech.

present Immediate. See note on 'presently', p.49.

sufferance Suffering.

born under Saturn And therefore of a saturnine disposition. That men's natures and fortunes were influenced by the star under which they were born was a widespread superstition of Elizabethan times.

goest about Take the trouble; literally, go the long way round.

moral Moralizing.
mortifying Deadly, destructive.
stomach See note p.48.
tend on Attend to.
claw Flatter, fawn on.
humour See note p.49.
controlment Restraint, check.
out We should say 'up'. Don John's rebellion is meant.
harvest i.e. benefit.
canker Dogrose.
blood See note p.49. Or, of course, he may be referring to his illegitimate blood. In any case this had much to do with his 'temper'.
carriage Bearing.
clog Block of wood fastened to an animal's leg to stop it wandering (or going through hedges). In the days of open field villages, clogs were much used.
the prince, your brother By referring to Don John's brother as 'the prince', Borachio would unwittingly sting Don John.
model Ground plan.
What is he for a fool What sort of a fool is he?
right hand i.e. right-hand man.
proper Handsome. Said sarcastically here, of course.
March-chick i.e. a chick hatched early in the year.
entertained for i.e. employed as.
smoking i.e. fumigating.
musty i.e. one that had been shut up for a long time.
comes me In Elizabethan English a singular verb before a plural subject is not an uncommon construction, especially where, as here, the two subjects are associated. The redundant 'me' is very common: it refers to something in which the speaker is indirectly interested and gives a more colloquial ring.
start-up Upstart. It made little difference in Elizabethan English whether the preposition or adverb came before or after the main noun or verb of a hyphened word, e.g. 'my downsitting and my uprising'.
cross i.e. thwart.
sure True, to be relied on (not referring to the news Borachio has brought).
Would ... mind! Then he would poison the lot of them!
prove Try, investigate.

Revision questions on Act I

1 What was the occasion of Don Pedro's visit to Leonato with his friends? What elements of danger are there in it?

2 Give an account of the plan proposed to win Hero for Claudio. Do you think more or less of Claudio for agreeing to it?

3 How does Don John find out about this plan, and what does he decide to do?

4 Give particulars of anything overheard in this act, and state how far the reports are true.

5 What is the dramatic value of the first part of the scene, before the entrance of Don Pedro and his friends?

Act II

Scene 1

At the masked ball after the supper at night Don Pedro woos Hero as Claudio and then hands her over to him. He does it so well that at one time Claudio thinks he has been double-crossed; he believes Don Pedro is wooing Hero in his own right. In this Claudio is encouraged by a malicious report from Don John and a jesting one from Benedick.

Benedick and Beatrice are both annoyed by what each says about the other when they dance together, supposedly unknown to one another. Don Pedro asks the others to help him to fashion a match between these two rivals.

Notice the meeting of Balthasar and Margaret, seemingly quite unimportant, but of importance later, in giving the play unity and credibility: also Claudio's willingness to believe that Don Pedro has tricked him.

I never can see him Yet it would appear that she has not seen him until that day! It is not important that this fails to agree with a time scheme. Shakespeare wrote for an audience in the theatre without a script, and it never occurred to him that people would study his plays from books and compare passage with passage.

my lady's eldest son i.e. a spoilt boy.

curst Bitter, cutting.

send you no horns See note on 'pluck off . . . forehead', p.51. The mention of the word 'horns' generally leads to this allusion, which seems to have been a constant source of amusement to Shakespeare's audiences.

Just Just so, quite right.

for the which blessing i.e. to be sent no husband.

in the woollen i.e. between the blankets.

in earnest of i.e. as a token that I am doing his work.

bear-ward Bear-keeper.

lead his apes into hell Apes frequently rode on the backs of performing bears. To lead apes in (Beatrice substitutes 'into') hell was the proverbial fate of an old maid, and as Dr Wright ingeniously suggested, a fit punishment for those who had escaped the plague of children in this life.

here's . . . maids i.e. among bad men.

Saint Peter for the heavens Saint Peter was reputed to carry the keys of the kingdom of heaven.

metal Material.

kind Manner, i.e. as a suitor.

important Importunate.

measure A slow and stately dance. The student will notice the pun with 'time', and with 'measure' meaning 'moderation'.

cinque-pace The first five steps of the galliard, a quick dance. The words are the French for 'five-steps'.

passing Surpassing.

a church Another reference to marriage.

your friend i.e. myself. 'Friend' was a stronger word in Elizabethan English than now.

So you Provided that you.

favour Face, looks.

defend Forbid.

like the case Remember that Don Pedro was masked.

Philemon's roof Jove (King of the Roman gods), disguised as a mortal, was received into the humble thatched hut of Philemon, after being refused hospitality elsewhere.

Which is one i.e. tell me what one of them is like.

clerk The clerk led the responses in the English church service.

do him so ill-well i.e. copy an ill-looking man so well.

dry i.e. old. A dry hand was supposed to be a sign of cold blood, that is, that the owner was too old for love.

up and down i.e. all over.

At In.

wit The word here and in Beatrice's speech below seems to have more the modern sense than that on p.52.

shall Must.

the 'Hundred Merry Tales' A book of cheap jests, popular in 16th-century England. Queen Elizabeth I is said to have enjoyed it.

only his His only.

impossible Incredible.

pleases men and angers them i.e. pleases men by his slanders against others and angers them by his insults against themselves.

fleet i.e. company (a metaphor continued in 'boarded').

break a comparison A metaphor from breaking a lance in tilting.

the leaders i.e. of the dance.

visor i.e. man wearing a visor (synecdoche).

banquet dessert (after the supper).

blood i.e. passion. Stronger and more specific than its use in Act I. The metaphor refers to the practice of witches in making wax figures of those whom they wished to injure, and then melting them or sticking pins in them to the accompaniment of curses.

accident Occurrence.

willow A symbol of unrequited love.

an usurer's chain Money-lenders often wore gold chains round their necks as a token of their business.

the post i.e. myself (who had nothing to do with it).

If it will not be i.e. if you will not leave me.

puts the world into her person Gives out that the world thinks what she thinks.

lodge Gamekeeper's cottage (which is bound to be lonely).

flat Downright.

to you With you.

misused Abused.

my very . . . her i.e. scold me for not answering her.

conveyance Dexterity.

terminations Terms.

all that Adam . . . transgressed i.e. the whole world.

Hercules The Greek god personifying strength, who performed twelve astounding 'labours', which Don Pedro has in mind at the end of this scene.

Ate Greek goddess of vengeance and mischief.

scholar Because Latin was the language supposed to have power in exorcizing evil spirits.

here i.e. on earth.

a man ... sanctuary i.e. hell without Beatrice is 'a sanctuary' compared to earth with her.

Prester John A legendary Christian emperor of Asia or, in later stories, of Abyssinia.

the Great Cham The great Khan of Tartary (China).

the Pigmies Supposed to dwell near the dominions of 'the Great Cham'. The people in Benedick's speech are described in Maundeville's travels or in the travels of Marco Polo.

Exit The exit of Benedick (and later of Beatrice) is dramatically necessary, so that the plot against them may be mooted.

use Usury.

put him down Upset him.

civil as an orange Punning on 'Seville'.

that jealous complexion Yellow is (or was) the colour of jealousy.

your blazon Your description of him, what you give him out to be. A heraldic term.

conceit Fancy, idea (of what he is).

all grace i.e. God, the source of all grace.

cue Naturally there are many theatrical metaphors in Shakespeare's plays.

fool Innocent.

the windy side i.e. the right side to drive care away.

alliance i.e. of families in marriage. The remark follows from Claudio's calling her 'cousin', and she (in effect) says, 'I have a new kinsman'.

the world i.e. the way of the world – getting married (implying not the way of the Church – renouncing the world).

sunburnt i.e. left on one side. There may be a connection with the churching service, for Psalm, 71, 6 used in the service, reads, 'The sun shall not burn thee.' The unmarried woman might therefore consider herself still left to be sunburnt.

heigh-ho for a husband A popular song.

getting Punning on the meaning of 'begetting'.

matter See note p.51.

star ... born See note on 'born under Saturn', p.52.

cry you mercy See note p.52.

By your grace's pardon Excusing her withdrawal to the Prince – the visitor.

just Exact.

breathing As a horse stops for breathing.

for you i.e. one with you.
watchings Keeping awake all night.
strain Lineage, descent.
practise on Plot against.
Cupid . . . archer Cupid's golden arrows kindled love in the hearts of those whom they struck (his leaden ones, hate).

Scene 2

Borachio outlines to Don John a plot to ruin the marriage of Hero and Claudio.

Notice the parallelism in the scenes. In the last scene we heard of a plot to make a marriage; this scene shows a plot to break one.

shall i.e. is going to.
medicinable Medicinal.
affection Desire.
thou Notice that throughout this scene Don John addresses his servant as 'thou', and Borachio addresses his master as 'you'.
temper Mix, make up.
estimation Worth, how other people esteem him.
vex A stronger word then than now.
intend Pretend.
like to be cozened Likely to be cheated. The word may have come to mean this from a form of confidence trick as common in Elizabethan times as today – pretending to be a man's 'cousin' (relative or close friend) – in order to impose on him.
instances Proofs.
hear me . . . Claudio He would call Margaret Hero and 'Hero' would call him Claudio (in order to allay the suspicion of any eavesdroppers). Shakespeare's plots do not bear close examination.
jealousy Suspicion.

Scene 3

Leonato, Claudio and Don Pedro let Benedick overhear them say how much Beatrice is in love with him. He is naturally amazed, and decides to be 'horribly in love with her'.

The three schemers arrange a meeting between the two at once, and Benedick speaks kindly to her and already imagines that he can 'spy some marks of love in her'.

It is interesting to see how Shakespeare's happy scenes often take place in the open air – in a garden or in similar pleasant surroundings.

here i.e. there and back again, in other words, 'I will do it at once.'
but I . . . again Much of the humour in the play comes from taking literally words that were not so intended.
***Exit* Boy** After this the boy is forgotten. He does not return with the book and try to find out where Benedick has gone.
tabor A small drum, used especially for accompanying the pipe.
armour i.e. suit of armour.
carving i.e. cutting (in his imagination).
orthographer Benedick seems to mean 'very finical in his choice of words'.
cheapen Make an offer for (as at a market).
noble . . . angel The names of two coins. The noble was then worth about 35p and the angel about 50p, but impossible to reckon in modern currency.
kid-fox Fox cub.
a pennyworth As we say, 'His money's worth.' Shakespeare's word is still used in the same sense, however.
tax Try.
To put . . . perfection To pretend that he is no good at it (out of genuine modesty, or fishing for a compliment).
nothing Punning with 'noting'. The pronunciation of the two words was similar in Shakespeare's time.
sheep's guts Used for stringed instruments.
dumps Now used only in the phrase, 'Down in the dumps.'
for a shift Such a qualified compliment could have given little satisfaction to Balthasar, if he was seeking one. See note on 'To put . . . perfection', above.
night-raven Probably a bittern or a nightjar. A bird of ill omen, hence, 'Come what plague could have come after it.'
O! ay The first part of Claudio's speech is spoken aside, the second part aloud.
Sits . . . corner? Is that the way the wind blows?
infinite Limit.
Faith, like enough This contrary suggestion lends credibility to the situation, and is meant to take away any suspicion Benedick might have that it could be a trap. As it is, he wonders.
gull Trick.

hold Keep.
halfpence Silver halfpence (the only kind) were, of course, very small.
ecstasy Here used of a frenzy that is not a happy one.
other i.e. other person.
alms Good deed.
daffed all other respects Put aside all other considerations.
contemptible Contemptuous.
hath ... happiness Is, indeed, outwardly well-blessed.
Hector Captain of the Trojan forces at the siege of Troy, and the most valiant of them all.
If he ... trembling Leonato speaks as the representative of law and order.
large Broad, free and easy.
counsel i.e. with herself, not from anyone else.
modestly Impartially.
another's i.e. the other's.
no such matter There is nothing of the kind.
merely Entirely, only.
dumb-show i.e. action without words. In pre-Shakespearian drama it was customary to present the plot of a play, acted briefly without words, before the play itself, e.g. in the play-scene in *Hamlet*. This was called the 'dumb-show'. It served the same purpose as the overture to an opera – to prepare the audience for what followed and get people in the right mood.
full bent Full scope, i.e. she does not love half-heartedly. A metaphor from archery, as a bow is bent to its limit.
censured Judged, criticized (not necessarily unfavourably).
reprove Disprove.
quirks 'Quips'.
broken on me See note on 'break a comparison', p.56.
sentences Wise sayings.
of her On her.

Revision questions on Act II

1 Mention all that you can remember in this act spoken by Benedick and Beatrice in scorn of marriage.

2 Give briefly in your own words all the bits of conversation between dancers at the masked ball.

3 What made Claudio doubt Don Pedro's good faith? Do you think that he was too easily impressed?

4 Describe the villainous plot proposed by Borachio to wreck the marriage of Hero and Claudio.

5 Describe how the parallel half-humorous plot of Don Pedro to make a match between Beatrice and Benedick was carried out, and what immediate evidence there is of its success before the end of this act.

Act III

Scene 1

The corresponding plot to make Beatrice believe that Benedick loves her is carried out by Hero and a gentlewoman, with corresponding success.

There is a very close parallel between the traps laid for Benedick and Beatrice, in method and in effect (see section on 'Characters' p.34).

Proposing Talking.
pleached See note on 'thick-pleached', p.52.
woodbine coverture Honeysuckle shelter or covering – 'the pleached bower'.
haggerds Wild, untrained hawks.
new-trothed Newly betrothed.
as full as fortunate Fully as happy.
Misprising Underestimating.
Nor ... no In Elizabethan English a double negative intensifies the idea, instead of logically cancelling it.
project Idea, projection.
How However.
featured Fashioned.
spell him backward Turn him 'the wrong side out', i.e. make good into evil, with a reference, no doubt, to witches, who were reported to say their prayers backwards.
purchaseth Earns.

not . . . cannot See note on 'Nor . . . no', above.
from Different from.
press me to death A medieval form of torture.
tickling A method of catching trout by the hand.
honest i.e. not affecting her character.
prized Reckoned.
argument The meaning here is nearer the modern meaning – talk, conversation.
name 'Report', i.e. people speak well of him.
are you Are you going to be?
every day In fun Hero takes the question in a different sense, and at first says, 'Once I am married, I am married every day', and then immediately follows up with the answer to the question as meant.
lim'd Caught (as a bird with bird-lime).
What fire . . . ears? Referring to the popular myth that when your ears burn it is because people are talking about you in your absence.
behind the back of such i.e. when people are talking behind the back of such a person.
better than reportingly On better grounds than other people's report.

Scene 2

A different Benedick, quiet and unobtrusive, is seen in conversation with Don Pedro, Claudio and Leonato. He has left them (on account of the toothache, he says) when Don John enters and accuses Hero of disloyalty. He tells them to put it to the proof by observing her chamber-window at midnight. Claudio says that if Hero is guilty, he will shame her in the church on the following day.

At the same time as Claudio and Don Pedro are exulting in the success of their plot to trick Benedick into marriage, they are themselves the victims of Don John's plot. The two parts of the scene make a striking contrast.

I do . . . Arragon Don Pedro had evidently changed his mind since the day he arrived, when he proposed to stay a month.
bring Escort, accompany.
bold with i.e. be bold enough to ask.
Draw it i.e. pull it out.
draw it A punning reference to the hanging, drawing and quartering of traitors.

fancy Used first with the meaning of 'love', secondly more in the modern sense.

slops Baggy breeches.

this foolery The way tourists abroad aped foreign fashions on their return, to let people see that they had travelled, was a constant subject of Elizabethan satire. Similarly today holidaymakers leave old labels on their suitcases.

by the loss of a beard Had Benedick heard that Beatrice 'could not endure a husband with a beard on his face' (II,1)?

civet A strong musky perfume, obtained from the animal of this name.

note Sign.

wash his face i.e. use civet.

lute-string Love songs were usually sung to the accompaniment of a lute.

conditions Qualities.

with her face upwards i.e. looking at her lover.

hobby-horses Buffoons. A wicker hobby-horse was used in the morris dance.

Good den Good evening, a contraction of 'God give you good even'. This greeting was given any time after twelve noon.

aim better at me Try to get a more correct idea of me. A metaphor from archery.

holds you well Thinks well of you.

circumstances Details, beating about the bush.

a talking of Being spoken of.

out In full.

that That which, what.

coldly Calmly, or, as we say, 'coolly'.

untowardly Unfortunately.

Scene 3

The constables of the Watch are detailed for duty. By good fortune they overhear Borachio tell Conrade of his perfidy (without understanding its significance) and arrest the two of them.

salvation The malapropisms of Dogberry and Verges are all part of the fun.

charges Duties.

desartless For 'deserving'.

constable i.e. foreman or sergeant. He is not trying to depute his own office; he is 'the right master constable'.

well-favoured Good-looking, handsome.
Both which Both of which (I have the ability to do).
vagrom i.e. vagrant.
bills A bill was a kind of halberd carried by the watch.
true i.e. honest.
make Have to do, 'meddle'.
more i.e. better.
present Represent.
statues For 'statutes'.
without Unless.
By'r lady i.e. the Holy Virgin.
church-bench Inside the church porch. There were no benches inside the church: people stood for church service.
coil bustle, stir.
Mass i.e. by the Mass.
my elbow itched Cf. note on 'What fire . . . ears?', p.62.
scab Punning on the obvious sense and on the word as a term of abuse.
pent-house Outhouse.
unconfirmed Inexperienced, not confirmed in villainy.
reechy Smoky, 'reeky'. Some painting of an Old Testament scene is plainly indicated.
Bel Baal, one of the false gods of the Old Testament.
cod-piece A bag shaped flap on breeches, tied with laces, corresponding to the flies on trousers.
possessed Informed.
Call up . . . constable Just as Dogberry had instructed them – 'An there be any matter of weight chances, call up me.'
lock i.e. a lovelock – worn by men about town in Shakespeare's day. They were generally tied with ribbon and worn behind the ear.
commodity in question Doubtful bargain, punning on 'in question' meaning 'under interrogation'.

Scene 4

Hero is about to dress for her wedding, but her heart feels 'exceedingly heavy'. Beatrice comes in, but it is a different Beatrice, with no tongue for wit. She blames her discomfiture on a cold.

This scene does nothing to advance the plot. It is a scene of atmosphere. Hero's feeling of suspense, a vague, unaccountable foreboding, before her wedding, is shared by the audience who (knowing what they do) sympathize with her the more.

It also gives further proof that Beatrice has unsuspectingly fallen a victim to Hero's trick to make her fall in love.

rabato Ruff, stiff collar.

tire Head-dress.

the hair Head-dresses were trimmed with false hair.

exceeds Excels.

night-gown in respect of i.e. dressing-gown in comparison with.

cuts Inlaid pieces on the edge of the garment.

down sleeves Ordinary sleeves to the wrist.

side sleeves Long wide ornamental sleeves hanging from the shoulder.

underborne Trimmed round and stiffened underneath.

quaint Delicate, dainty, 'graceful'.

saving your reverence i.e. excusing my mention of it (as if the word 'husband' was offensive). The phrase usually prefaced mention of unpleasant things.

wrest i.e. from its true meaning.

coz Short for 'cousin'.

Clap's into Let us start up with.

'Light o' love' A contemporary dance tune.

burden Bass part.

barns Punning on 'barns' meaning 'bairns', children.

'T is almost five o'clock The wedding custom in Elizabethan England was that the bridegroom went early to the bride's home and took her to church for the ceremony (hence the meal following the ceremony was called the 'wedding-breakfast'). At the end of the scene Claudio and his friends come to take Hero to church.

H Then pronounced the same as 'ache'.

be not turned Turk Have not taken a turn for the worse (i.e. a renegade from your vows of celibacy).

star i.e. pole-star. Margaret means that things are turned topsy-turvy, something that everyone relied on is of no use.

trow I wonder, declare.

gloves A conventional present between lovers (like flowers or chocolates today).

stuffed i.e. with a cold. Cf. Benedick's toothache.

apprehension i.e. wit.

wear it in your cap Perhaps thinking of the way a knight wore his lady's favour.

Carduus Benedictus Blessed Thistle, a medicine with a wide variety of uses and reputed to cure many ills. The pun with Benedick is the only reason for its mention.

moral Hidden meaning.
list Please. What Margaret says in effect is that she thinks that Beatrice is in love, but considers it wiser not to say so.
such another i.e. as you – he said that he would never marry.
meat Food (of any kind, not necessarily flesh) – as in the phrase 'meat and drink'.
grudging Grumbling. To 'eat one's meat without grudging' was a proverbial phrase for not grumbling at one's lot in life.
look with your eyes i.e. know a good man when you see one.
false gallop i.e. canter (which is not a true gallop). Margaret's tongue does keep a true gallop.

Scene 5

In long-winded, blundering fashion Dogberry and Verges try to tell Leonato of the arrest they have made, but he is in a hurry and cannot spare the time to hear their tale out. He deputes them to interrogate the two 'arrant knaves'.

Leonato's hurry – or Dogberry and Verges' incompetence – costs Hero her good name, but lessens the tragic effect, as the audience knows that it is only a matter of time before she will be cleared.

Marry An oath – literally 'by the Virgin Mary', but in effect no stronger than 'indeed'. Generally used at the beginning of a sentence.
honest ... brows A proverbial comparison of that time; presumably because the skin between the brows is open for all to see.
palabras Part of a Spanish tag (*pocas palabras*; few words) in use in Elizabethan London.
poor duke's For 'duke's poor'.
of On.
exclamation on He obviously means 'proclamation of', 'report about'.
to-night Last night.
excepting ... Messina Verges means 'Saving your worship's reverence', but says that Leonato is a bigger knave than the two prisoners.
a horse The 'a' is emphatic, i.e. one.
Francis Seacole The 'George Seacole' of Scene 3 could read and write, so Shakespeare probably intended the same person here and forgot the Christian name.
here's that Stage business is for Dogberry to touch his head.
noncome Dogberry confuses nonplus and *non compos mentis*.

Revision questions on Act III

1 Compare in detail 'the false sweet bait' laid for Beatrice with that laid for Benedick.

2 Describe the charge to the Watch and their subsequent arrest of Borachio and Conrade.

3 What is the dramatic value of Scene 4, where Hero is talking to her cousin and gentlewomen before getting dressed for her wedding?

4 Can you blame Leonato for not hearing out Dogberry and Verges at that particular time?

5 Mention any passage in the act which gives a sense of foreboding for the future.

Act IV

Scene 1

Claudio denounces Hero in the church, as he had vowed he would, and the wedding is broken up. Hero denies his accusations, but is stunned by the shock and swoons.

The Friar, convinced of her innocence, advises that she should be reported dead, while they wait to see how things turn out. Benedick's intuition at once asserts that 'the practice of it lives in John the bastard'.

Beatrice and Benedick, left behind, are drawn together by their common sympathy for Hero and their belief that she has been wronged. Benedick's advances are not repulsed and, at Beatrice's behest, he undertakes to challenge Claudio to a duel.

Notice how the tragedy of this scene is thrown up by being placed between the raw comedy of two Watch scenes.

The breaking of the love between Hero and Claudio in the first part of the scene is thrown into relief by the cementing of that between Beatrice and Benedick in the second part.

The more subtle comedy in the way Benedick approaches

Beatrice and ends up by going out to challenge Claudio in order to please her softens the tragedy almost as soon as it has happened. Their quiet conversation (in prose) relieves the tension – the audience can relax after the strain. The introduction of a comic element has the same effect.

Interjections ... he! As if quoting from a school grammar book.
learn Teach.
luxurious Lustful.
approved Proved.
No, Leonato This short line is emphatic. It demands a pause, and everyone is waiting to see what follows.
Dian Roman goddess of the moon, hence 'in her orb' orbit.
Venus Roman goddess of love.
wide i.e. far from the truth, wide of the mark.
True? This word follows from Don John's speech, and is no comment on Benedick's.
move Put.
to According to. The first question in the catechism is, 'What is your name?'.
then are you no maiden Since you lie about it as well.
liberal Open, loose-tongued.
misgovernment i.e. of yourself.
conjecture i.e. of evil, suspicion.
blood i.e. blushes.
on the rearward of After, following.
frame Shaping.
on Of. Cf. note on 'of', p.66. These words were interchangeable.
I myself ... her i.e. I valued myself nothing compared with her.
season Seasoning (to make it wholesome).
given way ... fortune Let things take their own course.
apparitions Appearances.
To burn the errors As if they were heretics.
hold Maintain.
reading i.e her face.
experimental seal The seal of experience. The verb 'doth' is singular because it is attracted to the noun 'seal', which intervenes between verb and subject (the relative pronoun 'which', with two antecedents).
Refuse i.e. excommunicate, have nothing to do with.
misprision Mistake.

bent Inclination to or disposition for.
practice Plot.
quit Rid.
throughly Completely, thoroughly.
mourning ostentation Show of mourning.
remorse Pity.
rack Stretch, exaggerate.
upon i.e. as a result of.
study of imagination Imaginative meditation.
liver Then considered the seat of the affections.
success The result or issue – good or bad.
levell'd Aimed; a metaphor from setting the aim of a gun.
sort Turn out, happen.
reclusive i.e. as a nun.
inwardness Intimacy.
justly Rightly.
Being that Since.
flow i.e. am carried along.
strangely they strain the cure They apply strange remedies.
prolong'd Postponed.
even Straightforward, plain.
thou Notice the subtle changes of 'thou' and 'you' in Benedick's speeches. Benedick here changes to the more friendly 'thou', but returns to 'you' in his next speech when he sees that his familiarity is not so well received as he had hoped. Then he has another try and keeps up the second person singular until the end of his advances. But in his last two speeches the personal pronoun is 'you', for they have an air of dutiful purpose about them – he is 'engaged' to do a deed and he will do it.
eat it i.e. eat your oath.
by it Benedick means by his sword.
to deny By denying.
I am . . . here My heart is gone, though you hold me.
bear her in hand Flatter her with false hopes.
Comfect Sugar-baby, candy.
melted into courtesies Developing the 'Comfect' metaphor.
trim Polite, careful; men say the proper thing, not anything which might bring trouble upon them and make them show their valour.
swears it i.e. swears it to be true.
engaged Pledged.
By this hand Beatrice's hand now.

Scene 2

Dogberry and Verges take Borachio and Conrade before the Sexton for their examination. The Sexton, who has heard how Hero was rejected and has died, realizes the importance of the information laid and gives orders that the two accused be taken bound before Leonato.

The audience is also made aware that 'Prince John is this morning secretly stolen away.'

in gowns The official dress of constables.
exhibition For 'commission'.
sirrah A contemptuous alternative to 'sir'. Conrade objects to the address and so answers, 'I am a gentleman, sir'.
defend Forbid.
go about with Outwit.
are both in a tale i.e. both say the same thing.
eftest For 'deftest'.
promise Assure.
naughty Good-for-nothing, a much stronger word than now.
that hath had losses i.e. whose status is better than it appears now.

Revision questions on Act IV

1 Describe the dramatic scene where Claudio repudiates Hero in church. What does it tell us about Claudio's character that he could save up his resentment for a public denunciation?

2 Outline the course of action proposed by the Friar, and say what you think of it.

3 Describe the interview between Benedick and Beatrice after the others have left the church. What is the dramatic effect of this conversation following the violence of Claudio's denunciation?

4 Give an account of the examination of Borachio and Conrade by the Watch. What is Shakespeare's dramatic purpose in sandwiching the 'denunciation' scene between the two 'Watch' scenes?

Act V

Scene 1

Don Pedro and Claudio say goodbye to Leonato. Leonato and his brother Antonio issue a challenge to Claudio. Benedick also comes in with a challenge for Claudio (though his motive for doing so is different).

The Watch then enter with Borachio and Conrade as prisoners, and Borachio confesses to his crimes. Claudio asks Leonato to impose what penance on him he will. The sentence that Leonato imposes is that on the following morning he shall marry Hero's cousin, the daughter of Antonio. Claudio naturally acquiesces willingly –

O noble sir,
Your over-kindness doth wring tears from me!
I do embrace your offer.

do suit with Are like.
And ... patience The incomplete line (three stresses only) emphasizes the passionate nature of his speech.
strain Pang.
wag Wag its head (as if about to utter some wise saying).
candle-wasters Students (burners of the 'midnight oil'), i.e. comfort from books (by men who have never felt grief).
passion Suffering, woe.
preceptial medicine The medicine of precepts.
wring Writhe.
advertisement (Your) admonition.
writ the style of gods As if they were above the cares of human suffering.
made a push at chance Pooh-poohed misfortune.
Are you so hasty now? On his arrival (I,I) Don Pedro said that he would stop 'at least a month'.
all is one It is all the same.
lie low i.e. be laid flat.
thou Note the pronoun, implying contempt (as if he were speaking to a servant).
to With, in moving to.
head i.e. face.
of a man i.e. by combat (in a duel).

nice fence Precise, accurate, neat manner of fencing.

daff See note on 'daffed all other respects', p.60.

men indeed i.e. who are indeed men – real men.

Win me and wear me A proverbial phrase referring to a man's conquest of a woman, but here applied to a different occasion.

answer me i.e. answer my challenge.

foining Thrusting.

weigh i.e. are worth.

Scambling Shuffling, walking along in mincing, affected fashion.

out-facing Putting on a bold front, staring people out of countenance.

fashion-monging Literally, dealing in fashions, implying constantly changing to keep up with the latest fashion.

cog Deceive, cheat, usually implying by flattery.

antickly In clownish, fantastic, grotesque fashion (as of boys who want to make a stir).

dangerous Threatening.

if they durst i.e. if it were not for the law.

wake Rouse.

Good day, my lord Notice how Benedick ignores Claudio and speaks to the Prince.

doubt Suspect, fear.

high-proof To a high degree. The metaphor is from tested (proven) weapons or armour.

as we do the minstrels i.e. drawing their bows across the strings of their instruments.

career Charge. We still say 'in full career'. The words in this and the next two speeches are from tilting (fighting on horseback with lance or trying to pierce a target with the lance).

staff i.e. of a lance.

cross i.e. across, implying a stroke without skill. If the staff of the spear broke at a full forward thrust it would split lengthwise and not across.

By this light A common exclamation of little significance.

to turn his girdle A proverbial expression, meaning to turn the buckle of his girdle to the back, and so put it out of the way ready for wrestling, i.e. to make ready for fight.

bless i.e. save.

Do me right i.e give me satisfaction.

protest Proclaim.

a calf's head and a capon Claudio is making fun of Benedick.

curiously Carefully.

naught Good for nothing.

'Just' See note p.55.

'a wise gentleman' Implying an old man full of cunning.
'hath the tongues' i.e. speaks foreign languages.
trans-shape Turn inside out, put the worst construction on them. Hero's equivalent is 'spell him backward' (note p.61).
the old man i.e. Leonato.
God . . . garden See Genesis, 3,8. A reference to II,3.
set . . . head Throwing Benedick's words back in his own face. See note on 'pluck off . . . forehead', p.51.
My lord Benedick now turns to Don Pedro.
pretty Foolish.
to Compared to (in size).
doctor Learned man.
soft A common exclamation of the time.
let me be i.e. do not worry me for a minute or two.
pluck up i.e. rouse thyself.
division Arrangement, sub-divisions.
well suited Dressed in different ways.
cunning Clever.
incensed Instigated.
plaintiffs He means 'defendants' !
specify For 'testify'.
bravely Finely.
me to On me.
invention Poetic composition.
pack'd Implicated, confederate, 'mixed up in'.
by About.
under white and black i.e. written down, or 'in black and white', as we say.
used Been used to.
thee Speaking to a servant, or one of low rank. Dogberry always addresses Leonato as 'you'.
God save the foundation! The usual formula of thanks for those who received alms of a religious house.
with Hero i.e. at, or in, her tomb.
lewd Base.

Scene 2

Benedick offers a reward to Margaret if she will help him 'to the speech of Beatrice'. When Beatrice comes, the first thing she wants to know is whether Benedick has honoured his promise to challenge Claudio (see IV,1). Benedick assures her that he has, whereupon Beatrice unbends and talks wittily with him, but her wit is not barbed.

Then Ursula rushes in with the news that 'Yonder's old coil at home': it has been proved that Hero 'hath been falsely accused', Claudio deceived, and Don John, 'the author of all', 'fled and gone'.

This scene does not advance the plot, but gives a sense of the lapse of time between Claudio's promise to visit Hero's tomb (Scene 1) and the visit itself (Scene 3). Nothing gives the impression of the flight of time so well as the passing of other scenes before our eyes. This scene also shows the progress of the love of Benedick and Beatrice.

come over Surpass. Also punning on 'stile'.
keep below stairs i.e. stay in the servants' quarters (instead of getting married and being a mistress).
it catches The greyhound is the only dog which can catch its prey in full career.
give thee the bucklers Own that your wit is better than mine. One would give up one's shield only when one was beaten and could defend oneself no longer.
pikes Central spikes of bucklers.
vice Screw.
Leander According to the classical story Leander used to swim every night across the Hellespont to see Hero at Sestos. On one of these swims he was overtaken by a storm and drowned. The story was told in Marlowe and Chapman's poem *Hero and Leander* (1598).
Troilus The pseudo-classical story of Troilus and Cressida was told by Chaucer in his *Troilus and Criseyde*, and Shakespeare himself has a play dealing with these two lovers. During the siege of Troy, Calchas, a Trojan priest, deserted to the Greeks, leaving his daughter Cressida in Troy, where she became the mistress of Troilus, one of the sons of Priam, King of Troy. At the request of Calchas, however, the Greeks negotiated the exchange of Cressida for a Trojan prisoner. Though she had promised to remain true to Troilus, Cressida soon forgot him and accepted a Greek lover, Diomede, and Troilus was heartbroken by her faithlessness. He was eventually killed in battle by Achilles.
pandars The word comes from Pandarus, Cressida's uncle, who was a go-between for Troilus and Cressida.
carpet-mongers Men dubbed knight for civil service in peacetime (and not war service in battle). The 'monger' is contemptuous.

blank verse This term was just coming into use (generally derisively) at the time *Much Ado* was written.
festival terms Choice language (fit for a special occasion).
came Came for.
his Its.
undergoes i.e. is under (or goes under).
subscribe Proclaim (literally over my signature).
politic Well-organized.
epithet Phrase, expression.
instance Remark, example.
in the time of good neighbours When men had no need to praise themselves, because their neighbours praised them.
clamour i.e. of the tolling bell.
rheum Tears.
Don See note p.47. The metaphor represents conscience as a gnawing worm. Cf. Mark, 9,44–8.
old coil An awful commotion – a slang expression.
abused Deceived.

Scene 3

Claudio here hangs an epitaph upon the tomb of Hero and sings it 'to her bones', as enjoined by Leonato in Scene 1.

None the less Claudio goes off thinking of his substitute wedding on the morrow.

Notice how the epitaph is distinguished from the play by its short rhyming lines. The word 'heavily', repeated in two short lines, breaks in like a chant or chorus.

monument i.e. family tomb.
guerdon of Recompense for.
Dumb i.e. dead.
goddess of the night Diana, goddess of the moon.
Till death be uttered i.e. till he has finished uttering his 'moan', or 'rite'. He first asks midnight to assist him, then the dead in their graves.
The wolves have prey'd Metaphorically as well as literally true.
Phoebus An epithet of Apollo, god of the sun.
Dapples ... grey A very beautiful line. Shakespeare was particularly sensitive to the beauties of the dawn.
several Separate, different.

weeds Clothes.

Hymen A marriage song of the ancient Greeks, though later personified as the god of marriage.

's Us.

this i.e. she did this one (Hero).

Scene 4

Everything ends happily. Next morning Claudio finds that the cousin of Hero whom he has agreed to marry is no other than Hero herself; Benedick and Beatrice want to make it a double wedding (not without a shrewd suspicion of how their love for each other has been contrived); and finally news comes that Don John 'is ta'en in flight' and brought 'back to Messina'. But, says Benedick, time enough for that tomorrow.

question Investigation, consideration.

faith His pledge to Beatrice.

confirm'd Steady, unflinching.

is your Is that your.

stand Agree.

attend Wait for.

hold my mind i.e. keep my promise.

Ethiop The usual word for a Black woman in Elizabethan English. Claudio is hardly complimentary to Leonato's niece!

Europa did at lusty Jove Jove (see note on 'Philemon's roof', p.55) changed himself into a bull to carry off Europa. The reference to 'horns' comes up again (see note on 'pluck off . . . forehead', p.51). The first 'Europa' means 'Europe', of course.

low Bleat. Benedick despises music ('I had as lief have heard the night-raven') and probably poetry, and in this rhyming verse affects what he considers a babyish and finical way of talking to Claudio. It is a mark of contempt.

got Begot.

owe you i.e. will pay you back later.

qualify Moderate.

largely In full.

familiar i.e. as if the occurrence were something familiar.

wit-crackers We still talk of 'cracking a joke'.

thou Benedick uses this pronoun to the Prince and Claudio, perhaps from a jocular contempt, or perhaps in the spirit of, 'Come, come, we are friends.'

in that Since, inasmuch.

denied Refused, given up.

double-dealer Punning on the application to marriage, a double-dealer in wedlock being unfaithful to his wife.

of my On my.

staff i.e. walking-stick. Old people's walking-sticks in those days were usually tipped with horn (and, of course, there is the usual pun).

brave Fine.

Revision questions on Act V

1 Describe the way in which Benedick delivers his challenge to Claudio.

2 Tell how the plot of Don John and his associates is brought to light.

3 In what spirit does Claudio set out to marry his 'new' wife?

4 All things considered, would you say that the play has a 'happy' ending?

5 Does the reference to Don John in the last few lines of the play make a good final impression, or is it an anticlimax in which no one is interested?

General questions

1 How does Shakespeare convey necessary information to the audience at the beginning of the play?

2 Mention anything in the plot which seems of little moment at the time but later is seen to have considerable importance.

3 How far is (*a*) the crisis, (*b*) the solution of *Much Ado about Nothing* due to chance?

4 Write a short critical essay on Shakespeare's use of his sources for *Much Ado about Nothing*.

5 'Although swift when its time is analysed the play is not so swift in its general impression'. Why is this?

6 Comment on the skill with which the various strands of *Much Ado about Nothing* are gathered into a dramatic unity.

7 Make a list of things (*a*) overheard, (*b*) received as confidential information, with comments on their effect upon the course of the play.

8 Discuss *Much Ado about Nothing* as a study in the power of report.

9 Mention any parts of the play too improbable for you to believe in.

10 What claims has *Much Ado about Nothing* to be regarded as a comedy?

11 Mention any contemporary (i.e. Elizabethan) manners, customs or amusements alluded to in the play.

12 'Shakespeare's excellence did not lie in his invention of plots.' Where did his excellence lie? Illustrate your answer from *Much Ado about Nothing* and, if you wish, any other play.

13 Does Claudio deserve Hero? Give your reasons in full.

14 In what ways are Benedick and Beatrice suited to one another?

15 Comment on Shakespeare's genius as a dramatist from his treatment of the Benedick–Beatrice scenes.

16 Do you consider that Don John or Dogberry has the more important part dramatically? Give your reasons.

17 What part is played by Dogberry in *Much Ado about Nothing*?

18 Write a paragraph on the character of Leonato.

19 Discuss the part played by any two minor characters not mentioned in these questions hitherto.

20 Point out a striking character-contrast in the play and work out the contrast fully.

21 'A good play has in it a variety of life and character.' Does *Much Ado about Nothing* meet this condition?

22 It has been said that though the play has a happy ending it does not leave us satisfied. Consider this view.

23 Why is there so much prose in *Much Ado about Nothing*? On what occasions and for what purposes does Shakespeare use verse in this play?

24 Mention two songs in the play and discuss their appropriateness to the scenes where they are introduced, with critical comments on their metre.

25 Give two examples of each of the following from the play, with a few notes if you think that they are called for: (*a*) simile, (*b*) metaphor, (*c*) antithesis, (*d*) punning, (*e*) malapropisms.

26 Does the constant antithesis and punning increase your enjoyment of the play, or do you think that it is overdone? Which persons of the play indulge in it most?

27 In what ways was Shakespeare's work influenced by the stage for which he wrote?

28 Describe an imaginary visit to an Elizabethan theatre for a performance of *Much Ado about Nothing*.

29 Which part in the play would you most like to act? Which do you think is the most difficult part to act? In each case give your reasons.